Advance Praise

"In their bold interrogation of the world's most ancient texts, Billy Carson and Matthew Lacroix have fearlessly peeled back the pages of time to bring us deeper layers of information - information which, if we take it seriously, defies everything we thought we knew about the origins and potential of human beings. If you are ready to have your deepest assumptions challenged, this epic journey is one you won‹t want to miss.»

Paul Wallis - 5thkind.tv - Bestselling author of "The Eden Conspiracy."

"My congratulations to Matthew LaCroix and Billy Carson on the publishing of their new book The Epic Of Humanity. In it they delve into the increasing evidence that ancient megalithic sites in many parts of the world were created long before the standard academic timeline of human civilizations being at most 6000 years old. Ice cores, oral traditions and ancient scripts tell us that prior to the end of the last ice age very advanced technological people created astonishing works in stone in different locations that were later inherited by cultures who repurposed them for their own needs. Matthew and Billy are helping to rewrite human history and to correct errors that standard academia has either ignored or dismissed. A brave effort and well worth reading and digesting."

Brien Foerster hiddenincatours.com

The Epic of Humanity

THE EPIC OF
HUMANITY

By
Billy Carson
Matthew LaCroix

4BIDDEN KNOWLEDGE

Copyright © 2023 by 4BIDDEN KNOWLEDGE. All rights reserved.

This book or any portion thereof may not be reproduced or used in any manner whatsoever without the express written permission from the publisher except for the use of brief quotations in critical articles, reviews, and pages where permission Is specifically granted by the publisher.

First Edition

ISBN: 979-8-9871224-2-6

LCCN# 2023947724

Although the author and publisher have made every effort to ensure that the information in this book is correct, the author and publisher do not assume and hereby disclaim any liability to any party for any loss, damage, or disruption caused by errors or omissions, whether such errors or omissions result from negligence, accident, or any other cause. Likewise, the author and publisher assume no responsibility for any false information. No liability is assumed for damages that may result from the reading or use of information contained within. Read at your own risk. The views of this publication do not necessarily reflect the views of 4biddenknowledge.

Books may be purchased by contacting the publisher and author at:

4biddenknowledge Inc
934 N University Dr #417
Coral Springs, FL 33071

4biddenknowledge.com

info@4biddenknowledge.com

Table of Contents

Advance Praise

Foreword

Chapter 1 – Lost Civilizations and the Ancient Timeline

Chapter 2 – The Anunnaki & Origins of Humanity

Chapter 3 – The Founders of Atlantis

Chapter 4 – Sunken Cities and Earth Catastrophes

Chapter 5 – Unveiling the Matrix of Reality

The Authors

Foreword

by Erich von Däniken

Every epoch has its own spirit of the time. This spirit is the just prevailing reason. The people who were ahead of their respective zeitgeist were mostly discriminated and despised. I remember Niklaus Kopernikus (1473-1543) who shattered the world view of that time by proclaiming that the earth revolves around the sun. Or Giordano Bruno (1548-1600) who proved that there were other planetary systems in the universe. Not to forget Galileo Galilei (1564-1642) who freed mankind from the conceit that the earth is the center of the universe.

Today all reasonable astrophysicists still proclaim that there is life out there, but no alien civilization has ever visited the earth. Billy Carson and Matthew LaCroix see it differently. They prove that the earth is not a closed system and contacts have very well taken place. Thus they contradict the straight prevailing spirit of the age. This needs courage. I recommend THE EPIC OF HUMANITY book as a groundbreaking look into the new reasoning and evidence. The old one has had its day.

Erich von Däniken Best Seling Autor Chariots Of The Gods?'

Erich von Daniken is arguably the most widely read and most-copied nonfiction author in the world. He published his first (and best-known) book, Chariots of the Gods, in 1968. The worldwide best seller was followed by 40 more books, including the recent best sellers Twilight of the Gods, History is Wrong, Evidence of the Gods, Remnants of the Gods, and Odyssey of the Gods.

His works have been translated into 28 languages and have sold more than 65 million copies. Several have also been made into films. Von Danikens ideas have been the inspiration for a wide range of television series, including the History Channel's hit Ancient Aliens. His research organization, the AASRA/legendarytimes.com, comprises laymen and academics from all walks of life. Internationally, there are about 10,000 members. He lives in Switzerland but is an ever-present figure on the international lecture circuit, traveling more than 100,000 miles a year.

This book includes:

- The largest collection of ancient texts ever contained in a single book that includes: Sumerian, Akkadian, Babylonian, Egyptian, Gnostic, Greek, and more.
- The 200,000-year timeline of humanity, from the rise of civilization.
- New archaeological discoveries, ice-core data, and compelling-scientific evidence to prove lost civilizations once existed.
- Detailed analysis of the Anunnaki and their role in human-Earth history.
- The future of humanity and transition into the Age of Aquarius.

Book excerpt:

Chapter 2:

The first place to begin when telling the story of The Epic of Humanity is read a passage from The Secret Book of John, which is a chapter from the ancient Gnostic/pre-Christian text known as the Nag Hammadi Scriptures, which was recovered in 1948 from a hidden cave near the Dead Sea.

The Secret Book of John states:

> *"At once the rest of the powers became jealous.*
> *Although Adam (Adapa) had come into being through all of them,*
> *and they had given their power to this human,*
> *Adam was more intelligent than the creators and the first ruler.*
> *When they realized that Adam was enlightened,*
> *and could think more clearly than they, and was stripped of evil,*

> *they took and threw Adam (Adapa) into the lowest part of the whole material realm."*

This profoundly deep quote is echoed by other esoteric texts as well, that each tell us the same thing: We are powerful beings created to be perfect. However, the important part of that text to also consider is what it says at the very end. "They took and thew Adam into the lowest part of the whole material realm." Think about what that means for moment. Due to intense jealousy by some of these creator gods, human beings were cast down to the lowest form of the material realm, known as the third dimension/third density. In fact, Yaldabaoth; one of the creator gods in the story goes on to state: "I am a jealous god and there is no other god besides me." But is Yaldabaoth really the one true God that created the universe as we're told?

As most can clearly see, Adapa and Adam are the same being with slightly different names used. This is a common theme that can be seen with certain heroes, gods, and individuals throughout history, such as Atrahasis and Noah. Once one recognizes this pattern, they're able to connect the names used by different cultures to identify the original source of those stories. That's why I hold cuneiform tablets to the highest degree possible and consider them the closest thing we still have to understand the truth of the past. As we go deeper into these texts, I will be including a god name table later in the chapter to aid in understanding the different names used by these deities or beings of antiquity.

Breaking down The Myth of Adapa further is begins by stating that a supremely intelligent being - known as Adapa, is created by a god named Ea. This human being is designed in the image of the Anunnaki, but due to his intelligence and perfect nature, he has the potential to become even greater than his creators. Sound familiar?

To the Sumerians, the term "Anunna" translates to mean: "those who from heaven to Earth came", or "those who Anu sent to Earth". While the term Anunnaki is technically Akkadian, it essentially means the same thing. Both terms point to the fact that these creator gods came here from somewhere else other than Earth. It doesn't state whether it was from another star system or simply higher dimensions, all we know is that it wasn't from our planet. So then, where did the Anunnaki come from?

Chapter 1 – Lost Civilizations and the Ancient Timeline

Matthew LaCroix

Ancient texts and legends from around the world speak of a time when highly developed civilizations once existed on the Earth that were eventually destroyed by devastating global catastrophes. These lost civilizations understood the secrets of energy, consciousness, and our forgotten connection back to the stars. Over time, much of their knowledge and the evidence of their existence disappeared beneath rising oceans, dense jungles, and sand swept deserts, until eventually they became considered nothing more than a myth by the majority of society.

For thousands of years, the enigmatic structures they built, ancient texts they wrote, and murals they left behind remained largely a mystery to most academics. Due to the technological sophistication and sheer size of many of these structures - such as the Great Pyramid of Giza in Egypt or Baalbek temple complex in Lebanon, most mainstream archeologists often *incorrectly* gave credit to later cultures for their creation. This caused a greatly antiquated and inaccurate version of human history to be taught in schools, due to a foundation that was based both on faulty data and biased logic.

The goal of this chapter (and book) is to resurrect both the lost story/timeline of humanity, along with the ancient wisdom from the past, and return that knowledge to the forefront of our collective society - in order to foster a *new* Golden Age in humanity.

The first place to start to achieve that lofty goal is to clear the air of many of the misconceptions and even deliberate *deceptions* that have been perpetuated by modern academia regarding the true age, influences, and sophistication of many of these ancient civilizations. This is a necessary step to take to fully understand the truth about our past. Those who are curious about the specific dates and time periods associated with these lost civilizations, I will be including a 200,000-year timeline I created, which I will thoroughly explain and break down as we go along.

The reason why there exists so much confusion surrounding ancient structures around the world and how they fit into the human timeline is due to *four-primary factors*. The *first* is due to the absence of writing on the walls of most of these megalithic sites. This made it very difficult to trace who actually built them and how long ago they were built. Those structures that did contain writings or symbols were most often the result of a later culture that found the ancient ruins and decided to build on top of them. This created great confusion for centuries over who originally built them.

The *second factor* is that it's extremely difficult - if not impossible, to accurately date rock. Only the organic matter found between the rocks can be radiocarbon dated to obtain a plausible age. This presents great challenges for accurately dating *when* many of the sophisticated-megalithic structures around the world were built - such as Sacsayhuaman in Peru, since they were often built with such precision that not even a human hair can fit between the blocks. This makes carbon dating nearly impossible, leading many researchers to falsely place them in the wrong time period in history.

However, that's not always the case. Archeologists working in the Anatolia Region of Turkey were able to obtain small amounts of organic matter from the megalithic pillars of Gobekli Tepe (due to being buried) that were carbon dated to be over 11,800 years old. This discovery has caused great controversy among many mainstream academics over its authenticity, since most are reluctant to change the old paradigm of history that confidently states that human civilizations are *only* 6,000 years old. This discovery would nearly double that number, and there is evidence to show that human civilizations may be far older than even that.

The *third factor* has to do with violent Earth changes and variable ocean levels. This will be one of the most discussed topics in the book, as it played a significant role in both the destruction of these ancient civilizations, as well as submerging many of their ruins beneath rising oceans. This created a great deal of confusion among most academics for how to accurately plot them on a timeline.

The *fourth factor* is much more deliberate and complex, and connects back to the old paradigm of history that I mentioned before. Some - such as myself, would even categorize it as a conspiracy theory. For those unwilling to accept such a notion, I highly encourage you to at least keep an open mind as you read this. The purpose of this book isn't to think for you, but to assist *you* in reforming your own thought-processes for what is possible. Henry David Thoreau once said: "Think for yourself, or others will think for you without thinking of you."

Despite the challenges that present themselves with the first *three factors*, I consider the *fourth* to be the major reason why the old paradigm of history still remains unchanged. Without getting too deep down the rabbit hole yet, it's important to understand that a small number of extremely powerful individuals and secret societies control nearly everything in our world today. That may seem like a bold statement to make, but for those who are "awake" and "aware" it couldn't be more obvious. This control over the events of history can be traced back to the time of Constantine I and the formation of the Holy Roman Empire around 330 AD.

The Stage Of Time by Matthew LaCrox

Constantine I (and his *superiors*) realized that the most effective way of controlling the masses would be through fear, religion and re-writing the historical narrative. Anything that didn't fit into the *specific* version of history and religion that was being conveyed by the Holy Roman Empire simply didn't exist, or was considered blasphemy. This was reinforced by large armies that were specifically tasked with seeking out any pre-Christian writings or monuments and either destroying them (Library of Alexandria) or locking those forbidden texts and artifacts away in secret vaults - such as the Vatican Archives, where they still remain to this day.

A famous quote that speaks to this truth was made by George Orwell when he famously said: "He who controls the past controls the future. He who controls the present controls the past." Remember those words of wisdom as you continue reading through this book. In many cases, it's necessary to completely start over with how to place many of the events and civilizations from ancient history in order to overcome the false programming that has plagued society for so long.

So then, let's start over from the very beginning using the most accurate and unbiased evidence to resurrect this lost story of our history. By following this dusty trail of evidence around the world, the nearly forgotten *Epic of Humanity* can finally become known once again. To do that, we need to travel back in time over 100,000 years ago to the very first city ever created on the planet known as Eridu. *This* is where our story begins...

Lost Civilizations and Ancient Gods

According to ancient cuneiform tablets from Mesopotamia - such as the *Sumerian King List* or *Eridu Genesis*, the entire human story began with the lowering of "kingship" from heaven in a city known as Eridu, located near the confluence of the Tigris and Euphrates Rivers in Iraq. The following is a translation of the *Sumerian King List* that was done by leading experts in their field. Pay special attention to the city names, rulers, and length of reigns mentioned.

The *Sumerian King List* begins by stating:

> *"After the kingship descended from heaven, the kingship was in Eridu.*
> *In Eridu, Alulim became king; he ruled for 28,800 years.*
> *Alalgar ruled for 36,000 years.*
>
> *Then Eridu fell and the kingship was taken to Bad-tibira.*
> *In Bad-tibira, Enmen-lu-ana ruled for 43,200 years.*

Enmen-gal-ana ruled for 28,800 years.
The divine Dumuzi, the shepherd, ruled for 36,000 years.

Then Bad-tibira fell and the kingship was taken to Larak.
In Larak, En-sipad-zid-ana ruled for 28,800 years.

Then Larak fell and the kingship was taken to Sippar.
In Sippar, Enmen-dur-ana became king; he ruled for 21,000 years.

Then Sippar fell and the kingship was taken to Shuruppak
In Shuruppak, Ubara-Tutu became king; he ruled for 18,600 years.

Then the Flood swept over."

Sumerian Kings List. Photo taken by Elisabeth Carson

One of the best ways to verify that historical information is accurate is to compare it to other ancient texts and cross reference the names and dates given. Before I discuss the specific cities, kings, and long reins mentioned in the *Sumerian King List*, I wanted to provide the translation for the *Eridu Genesis* cuneiform tablet for comparison. The *Eridu Genesis* states:

> "When the royal scepter was coming down from heaven,

> the august crown and the royal throne being already down from heaven,
> the king regularly performed to perfection
> the august divine services and offices,
> and laid the bricks of those cities in pure spots.
>
> The firstling of the cities, Eridu, she gave to the leader Nudimmud (Enki),
> the second, Bad-Tibira, she gave to the Prince and the Sacred One,
> the third, Larak, she gave to Pahilsag,
> the fourth, Sippar, she gave to the gallant Utu,
> the fifth, Shuruppak, she gave to Ansud."

The first thing to mention about the *Sumerian King List* and *Eridu Genesis* is the specific wording that's used at the very beginning of the tablets, where it references "kingship" and "the royal scepter" descending, or coming down from heaven. This is extremely important to consider when seeking answers for how human civilizations could have miraculously "sprung up" out of nowhere, and why the Sumerians are credited as being the *first* to discover mathematics, astronomy, astrology, agriculture, complex writing, the wheel, metallurgy, sailing, moral laws and rules, the first currency, and even fermentation. Essentially everything can be traced back to them.

The problem is that the Sumerians don't claim to have invented any of those things. Instead, they say that great beings referred to as the Anunnaki, or Anunna descended down from "heaven" to lay down the framework for a *new* civilization here. In a nutshell, that's what's meant by the word "kingship", meaning the blueprints and specific hierarchal structure for how a complex human civilization should be created on Earth, based on the Anunnaki's perspective.

Notice how each one of the cities mentioned in these tablets perfectly mirrors the other, which we know were all real locations that have been well documented and shown on numerous maps. These cities are referred to as the pre-diluvian cities of Mesopotamia, meaning *before* the flood.

In fact, the ruins of the city of Eridu can still be found left abandoned in the deserts of Iraq, and is rarely mentioned by modern academia. I for one, refuse to allow such obvious tactics of concealment and deception. Consider for a moment the idea that more than half a dozen cuneiform tablets - the *oldest* texts ever written, which describe Eridu as being the *first* city ever created on Earth, and yet the site remains abandoned in the middle of the desert, seemingly forgotten by the world.

Further evidence that supports the existence and importance of these ancient pre-diluvian cities - along with the role that the Anunnaki played, can be found in the Tablet of Shamash. The Tablet of Shamash is a cuneiform stone tablet that was discovered in 1881 in the Mesopotamian city of Sippar, Iraq. The tablet was found buried within an ancient temple known as the Temple of Shamash, which was dedicated to the solar god of Anu. Anu was considered the "father" of the Anunnaki - likely connected back to Source or Prime Creator, who ruled over all of heaven, which is why his symbol became the sun.

This role was eventually challenged by the second-generation god Marduk; known as Bel in Babylon, who likely assumed the role of the sun god Amon-Ra in Egypt.

One of the things that make the Tablet of Shamash so unique among other cuneiform tablets was that it was found inside a specially made terracotta coffer, which shows its level of importance to both the Sumerian, Akkadian, and Babylonian cultures. The reason it was so important to them was because of the specific depiction of the god Shamash (Anu) sitting on his throne – connected to the power of Atu (the sun/water disk), as well as the ancient message it contained.

The Tablet of Shamash: Wikipedia

The following is a translation of the Tablet of Shamash by experts at the British Museum. For those who want to verify the accuracy of these translations or looking for more information, they are available online at: https://www.britishmuseum.org.

Column 1 of the Tablet of Shamash states:

> "Shamash (Anu), the great lord,
> who dwells in Ebabbara, which is in Sippar,
> During the troubles and disorders in Akkad,
> the Sutu, the evil foe,
> had overthrown (them),
> and destroyed the sculptured reliefs.
> His law was forgotten,
> his figure and his insignia had disappeared,
> and none beheld them.
> During the distress and famine,
> under Kashshu-nadin-akhi, the king,
> the regular offerings to (Shamash) were discontinued,
> and the drink-offerings ceased.
> During the reign of Eulmash-shakin-shum, the king,
> the priest of Sippar, the seer, he entrusted it.
> At a later time, Nabu-aplu-iddina, the king of Babylon,
> the elect of Marduk, the beloved of Anu and Ea,
> the valiant hero who for kingship is well fitted,
> who overthrew the evil foe, the Sutu,
> whose sin was great."

The first thing to point out about this tablet is that the dwelling place/temple of the god Shamash (Anu) is the city of Sippar. This gives us a relative timeframe for when these events occurred, and provides evidence to show that they really did happen - since Sippar is mentioned as being a pre-diluvian city in both the *Sumerian King List* and *Eridu Genesis*.

The Tablet of Shamash depicts Anu sitting on his throne in front of the sun/water disk known as Atu. The Atu was an ancient Mesopotamian symbol representing the balance of the sun and the forces of nature. These cultures believed that these creator gods were so powerful that they played a role in the various cycles and disasters on Earth. This is shown with the symbol of "arms" above the Atu that can be seen *pulling* the strings and *interrupting* the natural flow of nature.

The tablet goes on to explain that a rival empire known as the Sutu, overthrew the city of Sippar and destroyed all the sculptures and temples there. This led to the offerings and daily praises to Shamash to cease, leading to a devastating drought in the region and subsequent collapse of the civilizations of Mesopotamia at that time. That's why there are such stark differences in the ages and time periods for these cultures.

For those who study these cuneiform tablets - and the roles that the Anunnaki creator gods and cosmic cycles played here, this depiction is extremely interesting and important to consider. It may help us to understand why in the *Atra-Hasis* tablets Enlil and Enki discuss creating a disaster on the planet to wipe away all of life. Could the *Tablet of Shamash* be related in some way? We don't fully know, but the evidence seems to indicate that. Also, notice that the symbol of the golden ratio is present on the tablet, thousands of years before the Greek mathematician Pythagoras discovered it. This would help to explain where all of this knowledge originated from, and why the Sumerians claim it was handed down to them from "above".

In 1963, a major discovery was made by Istanbul University and the University of Chicago when they found the remains of a massive astronomical temple complex in the Southeastern Anatolia Region of Turkey, called Gobekli Tepe. One of the things that made this discovery so unusual was that as they were digging down through the layers of soil and rock to reach the temple, they encountered strange artifacts that simply didn't make sense to them. Instead of finding subsequent layers of slow-linear progression from primitive hunter-gather groups that eventually developed into more complex societies, they found that the transition to a highly sophisticated civilization occurred almost instantaneously.

This prompted some archeologists and academics to begin to question the mainstream viewpoint of history, since it was clear that whoever had built Gobekli Tepe had done so with an incredible advanced astronomical understanding of the cosmos. Furthermore, the unusual artifacts I mentioned that were found in the soil layers around the temple proved that the culture who had built it possessed an advanced understanding of mathematics, agriculture, astronomy, and even complex laws.

This meant that the previous hunter-gather societies that occupied the region would have miraculously gone from being primitive to highly advanced nearly overnight. Just like the Sumerians, it seemed as though "other" factors were responsible for this rapid development. That's the reason why I feel so confident in the earlier interpretations I gave of the *Sumerian King List* and *Eridu Genesis*, since it matches perfectly with archeological evidence from these ancient sites.

This means that in order to understand the events of the past, we must simply start over and create a *brand*-new timeline for human history that objectively matches all the evidence. This timeline is based on a combination of evidence from tablets/writings, geologic and climate data, genetic information, as well the superior technical sophistication seen in many of the ancient-megalithic structures around the world

I would like to point out the dates shown in this timeline should be treated more as logical approximations; rather than facts, due to size constraints and a lack of concrete evidence. One thing is for certain though: the current timeline we're taught in school needs to be *thrown* out the window and replaced. While I fully admit some of the dates beyond 12,000 years are somewhat speculative based on limited evidence, it at least gives us a ballpark to work with for placing where these lost civilizations-major events likely occurred in the past. As time goes on, I fully expect some of these dates to change based on new evidence that's discovered. That's why I refer to it as a 'moving timeline' rather than a concrete one.

Remember, we must always keep an open mind to *adjusting* our perspective if necessary, or information becomes stagnant and outdated. That's what makes a good researcher who is seeking the truth. As many know, the inability to adhere to these core principles is the very reason we're stuck in this antiquated version of history today.

200,000 Year Timeline of Civilization

Time measured in Years Ago before Current Era

- **200,000** — Adapa origins (Mankind); City of Eridu founded (Eden); Bad Tibira & Shuruppak; Sumerian King List - First Dynasties Of Sumer
- **50,000** — Atlantis founded
- **40,000** — Pyramids of Khemit built; Atrahasis
- **12,000** — Younger Dryas Earth Changes / Great Deluge/Solar Outburst; Pre-Inca, Olmec, Aztec; Gobekli Tepe; Indus Valley Civilizations
- **8,000** — Kish founded – Second Age of Sumer (New World)
- **6,000** — Major climate disruptions; Gilgamesh
- **3,000** — Third Age of Sumer - Fertile Crescent; Dynastic Egyptian Pharaohs
- **2,000** — Ashurbanipal Library created; Roman Empire
- **Current Era**

Lost Civilizations span from 200,000 to 12,000.

Created by Matthew LaCroix

The first place to begin when discussing the historical timeline is to try to visualize what the ancient world would have looked like to our ancestors, and then try to figure out where each "piece" of the puzzle fits in based on the evidence. This is done using a combination of ancient texts, historical accounts, maps, ice-core samples, archeological evidence, geologic evidence, and studying ocean levels. What we find is that the Earth looked significantly different in the past then it does today...

Imagine the Earth 13,000 years ago in the midst of an ice age. The northern half of Europe, Asia, and North America is buried by one - two miles of ice that forms a nearly impenetrable wall. Deserts like the Arabian and Sahara are covered with extensive grasslands, and shallow seas with land bridges extend for miles beyond their current locations today. Large megafauna such as mammoths, giant sloths, saber-toothed cats, and dire wolves roam the wilds of the interior, while massive schools of fish, predatory sharks, and whales dominate the oceans.

Along the coastlines, Middle East, and throughout the warmer-equatorial regions of the planet, sophisticated human societies co-exist at the same time with more primitive hunter-gatherer communities. Island landmasses that eventually became submerged give rise to powerful-global civilizations that were *taught* the secrets of energy, advanced technology, and harnessing the energy of the planet.

These advanced civilizations understood the importance of solar and galactic cycles, vibration, mathematics, and how to obtain higher states of consciousness. This led them to construct massive pyramid-temple structures in order to harness and balance the electromagnetic energy of the Earth. This was based on a precise understanding of the ratios of the Earth, Moon, and Sun to one another.

This time period was known as the Pleistocene-Younger Dryas epochs, in which violent catastrophes occurred between 12,800 and 10,000 years ago, leading to a rapid melting of the ice caps, global floods, devastating earthquake and volcano activity, and massive wild fires across the planet. These disasters; commonly referred to as the 'Younger Dryas Earth changes' led to the destruction of these advanced civilizations around the world and caused a major reset on human progression. That's why they are referred to as the lost civilizations of antiquity.

Meanwhile, some of the hunter-gatherer communities that had co-existed at the same time survived the catastrophes in small numbers and later re-discovered the ruined remains of those lost civilizations. These more primitive societies (such as in the Amazon Basin) attempted to mimic the building practices of these ancient cultures and resurrect their knowledge but were largely unsuccessful. That's why this time period is referred to as the *Great Reset,* since humanity had to literally start over again.

Perhaps the best example to show this can be seen at Machu Picchu in Peru, South America where at nearly 8,000 feet in elevation, massive-perfectly carved granite blocks can be seen on the lowest levels of construction that are so precise, not even a human hair can fit between them. Meanwhile, built on top of those megalithic granite blocks are increasingly smaller and less sophisticated stones and cobbles that are held together using primitive mud/mortar. In between these two layers we find a level of construction that's clearly more advanced than the top layer, but less sophisticated than the bottom. So, what exactly does that tell us? It tells us that the ancient culture who built the lowest levels of these structures was the most sophisticated, followed by a second group who came along and tried to emulate them with *some* success. Then all of sudden this megalithic construction abruptly ended and a far more primitive technique was later adopted.

This abrupt ending to sophisticated-megalithic building can be seen in locations around the world from South America, Mexico, and Egypt, to Lebanon, Turkey, China, and Japan.

What that tells us is that after the first set of catastrophes occurred, a small number of elders from those advanced civilizations managed to survive, and attempted to rebuild. Then, another catastrophe occurred and they were completely wiped out. This is shown well on ice-core samples from Greenland, when during the Younger Dryas period, the planet underwent tremendous temperature and precipitation swings over a ~2,000-year period that strongly suggests that violent catastrophes occurred on the Earth during that time. For those looking for more information on these disasters and how it impacted these lost civilizations, I'll be going into much greater detail in Chapter 4 when I discuss Atlantis and the submerged cities around the planet.

In the case of Machu Picchu, it means that what we commonly think of as the "Inca" likely represented a later and much more primitive culture that found these megalithic ruins scattered across the highlands of Peru and attempted to mimic their building practices without much success. Therefore, the most important question is: Who were the original builders?

The indigenous elders of the Peruvian region refer to these builders as the "Viracochan's" led by the being/deity known as Tiki Viracocha. The myths handed down about this mysterious being claim he either arrived from the ocean, or from the bottom of Lake Titicaca. As strange as that may sound, it's important that I point out that besides Peru, the most sophisticated megalithic-structures found in South America are located near or around *Lake Titicaca*.

The famous carved "H's" and enigmatic "Gate of the Sun" found in Tiwanaku-Puma Punku have puzzled experts for centuries. Evidence shows that they were likely built by another mysterious culture that the locals of the region refer to as the Tiwanaku culture. The level of technological precision present in their construction is nearly unmatched anywhere in the world, and points to a highly sophisticated civilization that likely co-existed at the same time as the original builders of Cusco, Machu Picchu, Ollantaytambo, and Sacsayhuaman in Peru. Not only that, but they were likely influenced by the same being/deity known as Tiki Viracocha.

This common theme and description for the being Tiki Viracocha is also shared further north with the Olmec, Toltec, Aztec, and Maya cultures of Mexico and Central America with the "gods" they refer to as Kukulkan and Quetzalcoatl. That's why it's so fascinating to learn that the original name for this entire region was called *Amaruca* which meant: "Land of Plumed or Feathered Serpents". This greatly contradicts with the false narrative that society has been taught regarding the origins of the name America. As is commonly the case with ancient cultures of antiquity, we must remember that the term "plumed or feathered serpent" is more associated with important symbolism, rather than literal meanings.

The bottom line is this: Evidence clearly shows that human civilizations have risen and fallen based on various factors; such as catastrophes, droughts, and wars - and that over time, significant amounts of knowledge have been lost connecting back to the origin story of mankind, the identity of these beings/deities, and what our role is in the cosmos. As I mentioned previously, just because there exists artifacts or writings on or near a structure doesn't mean that culture was the one who originally built it. This is especially true in places such as the Giza Plateau of Egypt, where most of the pyramids and temples there were incorrectly named after pharaohs of the Fourth Dynasty, who had *nothing* to do with their construction in the first place. This false mentality is echoed by ancient sites across the planet and needs to be corrected based on all the evidence.

Now that we have a better understanding of what our ancient world looked like, and some the factors that went into the rise and fall of these civilizations, it's time to fill in the gaps for where everything fits in with the timeline. To do that, we'll need to start from the very beginning.

To determine where the beginning actually starts, we'll need to define what that means first. The specific way that I structured the timeline was based on when human societies became separated from hunter-gathered communities, followed by when the first cities were built. Thanks to the Sumerians of Mesopotamia, we have that information contained within ancient cuneiform tablets. For those curious, I will be extensively discussing the human origin story in the next chapter.

To place where 'our' story begins, we will use a combination of the human genetics' studies done by Lloyd Pye, the *Sumerian King List*, *Eridu Genesis*, *Atra-Hasis* and *Myth of Adapa*. According to the extensive research done by Lloyd Pye, the human genome and brain size underwent dramatic and "unnatural" changes somewhere between 200,000 and 250,000 years ago. On top of that, when you add up the length of the reins of all the kings mentioned in the *Sumerian King List* – along with the *Uruk List of Kings and Sages*, you get a very similar number. Just to keep things simple, I capped the timeline at 200,000 years - however, I fully recognize that some of this dating is potentially older than that.

Based on this correlation, along with other pieces of evidence that support it, I postulate that somewhere around 200,000 years ago the Neanderthal- Denisovan pre-human genetics on Earth were modified by a supreme group of beings/entities that call themselves the Anunna or Anunnaki. Humans were then created in 'their' image and likeness - just as Genesis states, to be physical workers on the planet. Not for gold mining, but for creating infrastructure and managing it.

According to the *Myth of Adapa* and *Eridu Genesis* tablets, the first city created was Eridu, followed by Bad-Tibira, and then Larak. Not only that, but evidence points to Eridu being the location of the famous "Garden of Eden" that's mentioned in the bible. The reasoning for that conclusion is not only because it was mentioned as being the first city, but the first city ruled by Enki in which Adapa lived. Adapa was considered the first **perfect** human ever created.

In the biblical version of this story, the "snake" tempts Adam and Eve with the knowledge of good and evil, before they are eventually cast out of the garden. Cuneiform tablets show that this "snake" was none other than Enki. Evidence to support that comes from the following quote from the *Eridu Genesis* tablet.

> *"The firstling of the cities, Eridu, she gave to the leader Nudimmud"*

Nudimmud was the first ruler of the city of Eridu and was closely associated with the god Enki. Some have even theorized that he may have been a physical incarnation of Enki himself. These names and shared characteristics varied depending on the time period and specific culture. This common theme is shared by many of the Anunna - especially Enki and Enlil, where they took on numerous names and symbols across countless cultures around the world. For those curious about these names please refer to Chapter 2 where I extensively discuss it and provide a god-name table.

The last two cities listed in the *Sumerian King List* and *Eridu Genesis* tablets are Sippar and Shuruppak. Not only is the city of Sippar mentioned in both the *Sumerian King List* and *Eridu Genesis* as existing **before** the flood, but it's also listed in another tablet I previously discussed called the *Tablet of Shamash*. In the Tablet of Shamash, Sippar is the focal point of the story, where the Anunnaki god Anu is worshipped daily in an ancient temple dedicated to him. Besides Anu, both Ea (Enki) and Marduk are also directly mentioned as being present which gives us clues to when the events occurred, and where to place Sippar on a timeline. Allow me to explain further.

Along with Sippar, the city of Shuruppak represents the end of what I call the First Dynasties of Sumer, which were wiped out due to a terrible catastrophe(s) referred to as "the flood" or "great deluge". This flood story is shared by ancient cultures around the world - through oral traditions and written records, and will be extensively covered in Chapter 4.

When studying ice core samples taken from Greenland, geologic evidence from North America, and historic ocean level changes over time, many experts believe that this catastrophic event(s) likely occurred at the end of the last ice age - roughly 12,000 years ago, during the time of the Younger Dryas period. By incorporating this important evidence, we're able to accurately plot when this flood occurred on a timeline, as well as where to place what I refer to as the 'lost civilizations' which includes: the Atlantean's, the Kemetians (Predynastic Egyptians), Indus Valley Civilizations, Pre-Inca cultures, and many others.

Some may argue that there isn't enough 'data' to accurately plot when these lost civilizations existed - and technically they are right, however, there are several key pieces of evidence that do provide us with compelling clues. The first piece of evidence deals with the destruction of Atlantis, which is based on the information provided by Plato in the *Timaeus* and *Critias*.

According to Plato, the island landmass of Atlantis was destroyed in a single day and night by violent Earth catastrophes 9,000 years before he existed. Based on historical data for when Plato lived, this would put Atlantis's destruction at roughly 12,000 years ago. Not only that, but when you consider the fact that this information was derived long before the theories of the Younger Dryas Catastrophes were proposed by academics, it provides credibility for the accuracy of this date for a timeline.

Expanding on this area further, each one of the lost civilizations I mentioned above created incredibly complex and sophisticated structures, many of which show signs of intense heat, vitrification, and severe erosion that is indicative of a massive-global event(s). This point cannot be stressed nearly enough, and provides overwhelming evidence to show that each of them was destroyed at around the same time period in history, by what can only be described as a global event. For this reason, we must draw a hypothetical line in sand, separating what are known as the pre-diluvian civilizations, from the post-diluvian civilizations.

For those seeking additional evidence regarding the timeline of these pre-diluvian versus post-diluvian civilizations, we find that evidence in the cuneiform tablets known as the *Epic of Gilgamesh*. While Gilgamesh may not have been alive before the flood, he was still a royal bloodline king of the city of Uruk, and knew intricate details about the events of the past – especially before the flood. In fact, the tablets of the *Epic of Gilgamesh* and the *Atra-Hasis* are the most complete records that exist describing the great flood, as well as the ancient cities that once existed in deep antiquity. The reason I put so much emphasis on the *Epic of Gilgamesh* is due to how closely it mirrors the *Atra-Hasis* cuneiform tablets, which were likely written thousands of years before. This helps to support its authenticity as a viable source of historical information. I'll be discussing who Atrahasis was and his importance to the story as we go along.

The *Epic of Gilgamesh* may be the most well-known of any of the Mesopotamian cuneiform tablets, and yet, it contains some of the greatest secrets of all. Many of those secrets were likely overlooked by most of academia due to the fact that it's still mostly considered a myth, and is quite lengthy (spanning 12 different tablets). However, hidden within symbolic stories and moral lessons are "gems" of truth that beckon to be noticed and understood.

The *Epic of Gilgamesh* was discovered in 1849 by Austen Henry Layard during an archeological dig of the Ashurbanipal Library in Nineveh, Iraq. It took several years to fully comprehend the significance of the discovery; largely because cuneiform writing was a dead language, but eventually it was realized that the Ashurbanipal Library represented the greatest collection of ancient texts ever recovered. Out of the thousands of cuneiform tablets that were found in the Ashurbanipal Library, The *Epic of Gilgamesh* was the first to be fully translated by Assyriologist George Smith in 1875 - more than 20 years after it was first found.

It was reported by his colleagues that as soon as George Smith finished translating The *Epic of Gilgamesh*, he was seen dancing around the room and shouting with excitement over what he had read. The reason that George Smith reacted in that way was because he was the first person to read The *Epic of Gilgamesh* in well over a thousand years. Imagine for a moment the feeling of translating and reading an ancient-dead language that was written more than 5,000 years ago, containing the Mesopotamian flood story, historical records of kingship, and the names of ancient cities from a time nearly lost to history.

When George Smith first translated the *Epic of Gilgamesh* in 1875, he was the only linguistic expert in the world that knew how to read ancient cuneiform. Since then, many experts have come along - such as Stephanie Dalley and Samuel Noah Kramer, to confirm the accuracy of his work and have gone on to translate numerous other tablets as well. However, out of the thousands of tablets that were recovered in the Ashurbanipal Library in 1849, only a few hundred have ever been fully translated. Today, most of these untranslated tablets are kept in dusty back rooms uncatalogued and nearly forgotten, with most of their secrets remaining hidden until a time when academia - and society as a whole, can fully recognize their significance to history. Now you may be asking yourself the question: What exactly does the Epic of Gilgamesh say, and what secrets does it contain?

The *Epic of Gilgamesh* begins by stating that Gilgamesh is a tyrant king of the city of Uruk in what would today be southern Iraq. This gives us a location for where story begins, and provides clues for how old the city is. Just like many other ancient stories from Mesopotamia, Gilgamesh embarks on a journey to gain wisdom, a greater understanding of life, and the secrets of immortality. This journey takes him far beyond the boundaries of Uruk, and into realms beyond this world.

Those who have read these tablets in school may remember how Gilgamesh meets a wild man named Enkidu, who travels along with him on his journey to battle Huwaha and the Bull of

Heaven. Enkidu (notice the similarities in the name) eventually dies from a disease sent as punishment by the gods, which leads Gilgamesh to seek out the secrets of immortality. This is the point at which our interest lies from a historical perspective to incorporate this information into the timeline.

Neo-Assyrian clay tablet. Epic of Gilgamesh, Tablet 11: Story of the Flood. Known as the "Flood Tablet" From the Library of Ashurbanipal, 7th century BC. Wikipedia

Gilgamesh was what's known as a demigod, which means that he was half-man and half-god. That's why I referred to him as a royal-bloodline king earlier, since he was considered a descendant of Dumuzi – 'the shepherd' of the Anunnaki. Not only that, but Gilgamesh was one of the last of his kind - known as the Nephilim in the Book of Enoch, which is why the "gods" become interested in him and the outcome of his story. In fact, the Anunnaki are directly mentioned *8 times* in the *Epic of Gilgamesh* tablets, where on **Tablet 10** it states:

> *"The Anunnaki, the great gods, held an assembly,*
> *both death and life they have established,*
> *but the day of death they do not disclose."*

Gilgamesh goes on to defy the Anunnaki gods and seek out immortality from the only man that was able to obtain it – Atrahasis. However, he's not called Atrahasis in these tablets. Just like many other ancient stories from Mesopotamia, numerous names are used for the same individual by different cultures and time periods. In this case, Atrahasis is referred to by Gilgamesh as Utanapishti: the flood-hero of Shuruppak. Atrahasis - also known as Utanapishti or Ziusudra, was a son of Ubar-Tutu and heir to the throne of the city of Shuruppak. You may recall that Shuruppak was the last city mentioned in both the *Sumerian King List* and *Eridu Genesis* that "kingship" was lowered to before the flood swept over.

Utanapishti or Ziusudra, was considered a direct descendant of Enki himself. That's the reason why he was secretly warned by Enki to build a bitumen-reinforced cedar boat before the deluge occurred, in order for his family bloodline to be preserved. This helps to explain why Utanapishti shares so many similarities with the biblical story of Noah, since it was originally based on his account in both the *Atra-Hasis* and *Epic of Gilgamesh*.

After its discovered that Utanapishti survived the deluge, he's given immortality by the Anunna (Council of Twelve), which - according to the cuneiform tablet known as the *Death of Biligames*, is the last time a human was given this gift. Reading a short excerpt from the *Death of Biligames* tablet it states:

> *"After the Assembly (Council of Twelve)*
> *had made the deluge sweep over,*
> *Ziusudra, one of mankind, still lived!*
> *From that time "we" (the Anunna)*
> *swore that mankind should **not** have eternal life."*

Continuing on with Tablet 11 of the *Epic of Gilgamesh*, Gilgamesh learns of Utanapishti's location at "the ocean at the end of the world" or across the "waters of death" and travels there to seek his council regarding the secrets of immortality. After carefully studying the wording used in this description, I've concluded that this reference most likely pertains to the realm(s) of the underworld. Perhaps that's the only way for a mortal being to be able to obtain immortality - but at great cost...

Tablet 11 of the Epic of Gilgamesh states:

> *"I look at you, Utanapishti, **your** form is no different, you are just like me,*
> *How was it you stood with the gods in assembly?*
> *How did you find the life eternal?'*
> *Said Utanapishti to him, to Gilgamesh:*
> *'Let me disclose, Oh Gilgamesh, a matter most secret,*

> *to you I will tell a mystery of gods.*
> *'The town of Shuruppak, a city well known to you,*
> *which stands on the banks of the Euphrates.*
> *This city was old – the gods once were in it –*
> *when the great gods decided to send down the deluge."*

Utanapishti goes on to tell Gilgamesh the story of the great deluge which destroyed what was known as the "old world", leading to the destruction of most - if not all of the ancient civilizations on the Earth at that time. Shuruppak is mentioned because it was one of the last cities that kingship was lowered to by the Anunnaki in which Utanapishti and his father - Ubara-Tutu, were rulers of. That's why the description of the flood is so similar in both the *Atra-Hasis* and *Epic of Gilgamesh* tablets, since Utanapishti was one of the only humans who survived to tell about it.

The other piece of information revealed in Tablet 11 of The *Epic of Gilgamesh* that is of great interest to me from a timeline/research perspective is what Utanapishti says about the city of Shuruppak when he states:

> *"This city was old – the **gods** once were **in** it"*

According to the *Epic of Gilgamesh* - as well as other Mesopotamian tablets, after the Anunnaki gods brought on the deluge, they decided to leave our realm (in physical form) due to how destructive and traumatizing the event was. Many of the Anunna felt the flood was a mistake, and greatly regretted allowing such an atrocity to occur. That means that – according to cuneiform records, Shuruppak was the last city in which the Anunnaki existed on Earth in physical form. Perhaps that's why we see such a stark contrast between the level of knowledge and sophistication with the pre-diluvian civilizations, versus the post-diluvian civilizations that came later.

In Chapter 4 I will be including the full translation for Tablet 11 -telling the story of the flood, but for now we will skip ahead to the end of the tablet where it states:

> *"Ea opened his mouth to speak,*
> *saying to the hero Enlil:*
> *'You, the sage of the gods, the hero,*
> *how could you lack counsel and bring on the Deluge?*
> *In the past, Utanapishti was a mortal man,*
> *but now he and his wife shall become like us gods!*
> *Utanapishti shall dwell far away,*
> *where the rivers flow forth!"*

Gilgamesh learns from Utanapishti that he will never be able to gain eternal life as long as he is a mortal man. Gilgamesh goes on to challenge Utanapishti's assertion whereby he is given several tests; such as not sleeping for a week, but ultimately fails at each one. Utanapishti eventually advises the boatman (ferry for the underworld) to take Gilgamesh back home, where he returns to Uruk empty-handed and disappointed. The tablets end with Enlil stating that it was never in Gilgamesh's destiny to gain eternal life. Instead, Gilgamesh was given the divine 'kingship' to rule over the city of Uruk by the Anunnaki.

The information contained within the *Epic of Gilgamesh* helps to bridge an important gap between understanding the events that occurred both before, and after the deluge. We learn that Gilgamesh is a post-diluvian king of the city of Uruk, and that Utanapishti was a pre-diluvian king of the city of Shuruppak. This provides evidence to back up the conclusions presented in my timeline regarding the different "epochs" or dynasties that occurred with these cultures, and how some - such as the Sumerians, were often separated by thousands of years.

Going even a step further, in the *Epic of Gilgamesh* we also find out that during his journey into the underworld, Gilgamesh meets the spirit of Etana. For those who don't know, Etana was chosen by the Anunnaki to be the "architect" of the 'New World' after the deluge destroyed everything. That's why the city of Kish is considered the very first city that emerged after the events of the flood. The fact that Gilgamesh mentions seeing the spirit of Etana in the underworld means that Etana was alive during an earlier time period than him. This helps us to separate when these events fall on a historical timeline.

The *Legend of Etana* is a set of cuneiform tablets that was recovered from the Ashurbanipal Library in 1849. It contains some of the most important clues for understanding the events that occurred immediately after the deluge - describing the first city that kingship was re-lowered to, and the influences of the Anunnaki/Igigi. Pay close attention to the specific wording used regarding the significance of the city of Kish, and how it describes the role that the Anunnaki play(ed) here.

Tablet 1 of the *Legend of Etana* begins with:

> *"They planned a city*
> *The gods laid its foundations*
> *They planned the city of Kish*
> *The Igigi founded its brickwork*
> *"Let him be their (the people's) shepherd,*
> *"Let Etana be their architect..."*
> *The Great Anunnaki gods 'ordainers of destinies,'*
> *Sat taking their counsel concerning the land,*

The creators of the four world regions, establishers of all physical form."

According to Tablet 1 of the *Legend of Etana*, after the deluge destroyed the infrastructure of the 'old world' kingship had to be re-lowered again by the Anunna to the city of Kish. Not only that, but the tablet opens by stating that the Anunnaki themselves planned the design of the city, and that the Igigi were the ones who actually built it. One has to wonder if the lack of humans after the deluge was the reason that the Igigi were tasked with building the city, instead of them. The big question is: How much time went by between the events of the deluge and the re-lowering of kingship to Kish? Was it hundreds of years? Or perhaps thousands? We may never fully know, but we do have clues.

The *Legend of Etana* goes on to describe how Etana - a royal bloodline descendant of the Anunnaki, was chosen to rule over the remaining people of the region. Based on the information contained within the *Epic of Gilgamesh*, we know that these events occurred before Gilgamesh was a king of the city of

Uruk, but after the destructive events of the deluge. That's why I decided to place these events somewhere around 10,000 years ago on the historical timeline.

The last thing I want to mention about this tablet is what it states towards the end when it says:

> "The Great Anunnaki gods... **establishers of all physical form.**"

If we were to take this passage literally - which I believe we should, it means that the Anunnaki are more far powerful than most realize. Similar to us, they are creator beings, but immortal and superior in many ways. After all, we were created in their image and likeness, but with far more empathy and compassion towards others in most cases.

If you consider that the Anunna had the ability to create human beings from stealing the life-force of an Igigi god, than why would they not have the ability to create other forms of life as well? Remember, it's clearly stated in these tablets that the Anunna deliberately caused the deluge in order to cleanse the planet of humans and start over again. That's why I try to always keep an open mind when studying this information so that I don't limit myself to what is possible.

I will leave the reader to think deeply about the implications of what this information means on a higher-level perspective for evolution and the origins of life. It seems the more I study these tablets, the more secrets they eventually reveal to me. Perhaps that's the purpose all along with the complexity in which they were written.

Now that we've covered the immediate events after the deluge and the re-lowering of kingship to Kish, it's time to move on to explain the events that occurred afterwards. When one studies this information, they find a distinct separation between the time period of Etana/Gilgamesh, and the later Sumerian/Akkadian/Babylonian civilizations of Mesopotamia. This is also true for many other ancient societies around the world as well - such as the Egyptians, Maya, Pre-Aztec, Inca, and many others. That's why I label these earlier cultures as the "lost civilizations" of history, since it's clear that they became less and less advanced as time went on.

It seems the reason for this is that a second disaster occurred that greatly disrupted these cultures. However, instead of a deluge/coronal mass ejection from the sun, it was likely a series of devastating droughts and fires brought on by significant climate changes to the region. Not only that, but these climate fluctuations likely played a major role in later time periods as well.

This would help to explain why there is such a disconnect between these earlier cultures, and why they seem to have 'fallen' from a state of sophistication and higher knowledge, to a more primitive state over time. This information means that the story of humanity is far older and more complex than modern academia is willing to admit.

The remaining 4,000 years of human history largely features the gradual collapse of the remaining ancient civilizations from antiquity, leading to the rise of powerful war empires - such as the Babylonian, Ottoman, and Roman Empires. Those that didn't succumb to devastating climate disruptions or large-scale regional wars eventually became corrupt, or were hunted down for destruction and eradication. Saint Patrick's Day and the burning of the Library of Alexandria are just a couple of examples of this.

Instead of the foundations of truth and knowledge being at the forefront of society, deception, fear, and organized conspiracies became the dominant tactic used by corrupted secret societies that gained control of most of our world. Those groups eventually became known as the Illuminati or Cabal, who used the monetary systems of the planet to control and puppeteer other nations to fulfill their specific agendas.

This downward spiral of knowledge and spiritual connection within humanity largely continues to this day, and should act as a stark warning for the direction we're headed in. If society continues to allow darkness to wield control over our destiny, we too will disappear like so many that came before us. It's not simply that learning about history is informative and interesting, but it fundamentally changes how one perceives our origins, responsibilities here, and the path we'll take in the future.

Remember, we each have a choice to make here based on the law of free will and deciding to follow a path of higher consciousness. Will we make it to the Golden Age of Aquarius? Only time will tell. For now, I am confident that those reading these words will someday remember the role that they play here, and will help to ensure our path back to where we started.

Chapter 2 –
The Anunnaki &
Origins of Humanity

By Matthew LaCroix

What do you feel when you stare up into the vast cosmos on a clear night? Curiosity? Perhaps wonder? With billions of star systems and earth-like worlds found throughout the Milky Way Galaxy, the two questions most often asked are, "Are we alone in the universe, and what is our purpose here?"

Some may be surprised to learn that those answers can be found within some of the oldest texts ever written, which often contain a significantly different version of the human origins story and the events of the past than we've been taught in school. Once one reads these important texts and studies the countless megalithic ruins left behind by these ancient cultures, their perspective about history, the nature of reality and whether we are alone in the universe often becomes much clearer. Quickly, you begin to realize that humanities epic is one of the *greatest* stories ever told.

What's even more shocking is that most of society is completely unaware of the existence of these ancient texts and that an organized effort is still in place to prevent this vital information from reaching the masses. That quest of teaching others and spreading knowledge led me to collaborate with another important researcher named Billy Carson, and together, we're working to resurrect the truth about our past so that it can finally be known once again.

The commonly held belief that the entire human origin story is derived from nothing more than random evolutionary changes in primates; based on a survival of the fittest mentality - with no outside influences, never sat well with me. I just couldn't understand how if Homo sapiens came from apes, then why don't we observe apes that are still undergoing this evolutionary change? Yet today, not one ape has ever been documented undergoing these evolutionary changes. Furthermore, why do humans only have 46 chromosomes, while most common primates have 48?

But beyond those mysterious anomalies found within our DNA, the most significant piece of evidence that strongly suggests that humans were genetically modified by outside influences in the past comes from the chakra centers of energy found along the spinal cord. Ancient Egyptian, Hindu, Mesopotamian, and Asian cultures have all extensively discussed the importance of the chakra system and pineal gland (known as the third-eye) found within the human body, explaining the significance they play for achieving higher states of consciousness and energy. In a nutshell, this chakra system found within us would have been completely *impossible* to have been created solely by natural evolution.

According to the Gnostics, the world we observe is in many ways an illusion within the third-dimension realm of what is known as the physical reality. That reality (for us) is based entirely on the seven colors of the visible light spectrum. Those seven colors (red, orange, yellow, green, blue, indigo, and violet) define everything in reality for us. Think about when you observe the vibrant green leaves on a tree, or the aqua blue color of the ocean, those colors are based on a manifestation of a certain vibration frequency. That means, that each of the seven colors that make up our physical reality is based on *specific* vibration frequencies.

Homo sapiens are the only species on Earth; out of billions, that have this chakra system found within us. Even more impressive, is that our seven chakras exactly mimic the vibrational frequency of the seven colors of the visible light spectrum. But how could that be? Just a coincidence? When a person begins to awaken to higher states of consciousness, their energetic-vibrational state changes along with it, allowing them to increase their conscious awareness of reality. That means that humans in many ways are *light beings,* since we have been perfectly designed to reflect the colors of the light spectrum for the means of achieving our highest state of energy here - known as Kundalini or the coiled serpent energy within.

Since consciousness and the soul is non-physical, it means that human beings here are having a physical experience that is entirely based on the invisible strings of vibrating energy that make up what we think of as the nature of reality. This theoretical concept is known as super string theory. Breaking that concept down further, it means the humans have the ability - built in, to ascend their consciousness and energy to eventually become powerful creator gods here. Let's go further and expand on this concept.

In order to break free of this conditioning that seeks to control us, we *must* tear down the antiquated and deceptive means by which we have been falsely programmed - to allow higher states of consciousness to rule our perceptions. From ancient history and human origins, to dimensions, timelines, and even the existence of sentient life in the universe, this information has been carefully guarded and hidden by certain secret societies and powerful empires for thousands of years.

This challenging and sometimes painful process requires an open and objective mind that is willing to re-learn certain concepts and ideas in pursuit of the truth. A quote that speaks to the importance of obtaining higher states of knowledge and awareness was made by Eckhart Tolle when he said: "The awakening of consciousness is the next evolutionary step for mankind".

Instead of living in a world focused on materialism, the accumulation of wealth, and distraction, we should look beyond those clever illusions to find our true purpose here. So now, the most important question then becomes: "Where do we come from?"

The first place to begin when telling the story of *The Epic of Humanity* is read a passage from *The Secret Book of John*, which is a chapter from the ancient Gnostic/pre-Christian text known as the Nag Hammadi Scriptures, which was recovered in 1948 from a hidden cave near the Dead Sea.

The Secret Book of John states:

> "At once the rest of the powers became jealous.
> Although Adam (Adapa) had come into being through all of them,
> and they had given their power to this human,
> Adam was more intelligent than the creators and the first ruler.
> When they realized that Adam was enlightened,
> and could think more clearly than they, and was stripped of evil,
> they took and threw Adam (Adapa) into the lowest part of the whole material realm."

Codex II, one of the most prominent Gnostic writings found in the Nag Hammadi library, which contains the end of the Gospel of Thomas and the beginning of the Apocryphon of John. Wikipedia

This profoundly deep quote is echoed by other esoteric texts as well, that each tell us the same thing: We are powerful beings *created* to be <u>perfect</u>. However, the important part of that text to also consider is what it says at the very end. "They took and thew Adam into the lowest part of the whole material realm." Think about what that means for moment. Due to intense jealousy by *some* of these creator gods, human beings were cast down to the lowest form of the material realm, known as the third dimension/third density. In fact, Yaldabaoth; *one* of the creator gods in the story goes on to state: "I am a jealous god and there is no other god besides me." But is Yaldabaoth really the one true God that created the universe as we're told?

For those who study these texts, and then compare to even older writings, such as the *Atra-Hasis* or *Enuma Elish*, they find strong comparisons to Yaldabaoth being the Sumerian equivalent of Enlil, who seems to also play the role of Yahweh in the Old Testament of the Bible. This is a key concept to understand as we go forward.

It's important that I point out that in many cases these stories are derived from much older tales, often spanning multiple epochs and time periods. Just because a particular story is written down by a certain dynasty or culture, doesn't necessarily mean it happened to them. Often times these stories are carried down for thousands of years prior due to how important they were. This is also true of many ancient megalithic structures as well, where later civilizations were incorrectly given credit for their creation.

So, now you may be wondering to yourself: "Who is Enlil and what part does he play in the human origin story?" In order to find the truth about our past, we must go back to the very beginning to the oldest texts ever written, known as Mesopotamian cuneiform tablets. In many ways, the origin story of human beings revolves around a very specific group of deities or gods that the Sumerians called The Anunnaki. This is where *The Epic of Humanity* begins.

Creator Gods and Human Origins

In 1849, an archeologist named Austen Henry Laird made a startling discovery in the ruins of the city of Nineveh, Iraq when he found a large cache of rare cuneiform tablets. Austen didn't know at the time, but he had stumbled upon the *greatest* libraries ever amassed in history - known as The Library of Ashurbanipal. The famous writer H.G. Wells would go on to call the Ashurbanipal Library: "the most precious source of historical material in the world."

Ashurbanipal was a king and high priest of the Neo-Assyrian Empire who ruled over the city of Nineveh - and surrounding region from 669-631 BC. He was considered the fourth king of the Sargonid dynasty and son of the famous ruler known as Esarhaddon. Ashurbanipal states in his writings that he became enamored by the contents of these cuneiform tablets and felt that they were the most important texts ever written by mankind. He ordered his armies to search ancient cities and ruins all across Mesopotamia in order to locate and obtain them. Before he died, Ashurbanipal managed to collect over

30,000 cuneiform tablets and placed them in a large library he had built in the royal palace.

After they were unearthed in 1849, the tablets were eventually moved to Oxford, England and housed in the British Museum where they still remain today. Unfortunately, most of the 30,000 tablets were never fully translated and those that were, often became labeled as nothing more than myths or allegorical stories by mainstream experts.

For those who don't know, cuneiform is a style of writing in which a clay brick or stone has a message etched into it, and then is often heated to preserve it. This brilliantly thought-out writing style by the Sumerians, Akkadians, and Babylonians meant that their message could be preserved for far longer than paper (which only lasts 500-1000 years) or any other form of writing. The only problem was that no one at the time knew how to translate them, since Sumerian and Akkadian were considered dead languages. That all changed in the 1870's with a man named George Smith.

George Smith was an expert Assyriologist that extensively studied ancient Mesopotamian cultures - and at that time, was the *only* person in the world that knew how to translate cuneiform tablets. However, even George Smith was unprepared for what he was about to discover. As he sorted through hundreds of tablets, brushing away the accumulated dirt and dust from thousands of years, the realization of what he was looking at began to become clearer.

Instead of just reading about the daily lives of the Sumerians, Akkadians, and Babylonians - explaining their agricultural practices, trading, and laws that made up their society, George Smith was stunned to find that the tablets contained heroic stories of giant kings, ancient gods known as the Anunna/Anunnaki, and extensive details about the origin story of humanity. Above all, George Smith recognized that the Anunnaki were the key players to truly understanding our past.

This information greatly contradicts certain mainstream academics and naysayers who claim that Zechariah Sitchin made up the term "Anunnaki" and that the entire story is a myth. This couldn't be further from the truth, as Assyriologist expert's Stephanie Dalley and Samuel Noah Kramer later verified George Smith's translations in the 1960's and 1970's and confirmed their accuracy. As I pointed out, these tablets were translated well over 100 years prior to Sitchin by the top Assyriologist in the world at the time. Having said that though, I'd like to point out that I don't agree with every interpretation and translation that was done by Sitchin. Especially regarding the purpose of why humans were created, and the significance of the number 3,600.

Of all the cuneiform tablets recovered across Mesopotamia in the last several hundred years, arguably the most significant of those came from the Ashurbanipal Library. Famous ancient texts such as The *Epic of Gilgamesh*, *Myth of Adapa*, *Enuma Elish*, or *Atra-Hasis* were all found in this important library. Yet - sadly, most of society is completely unaware of these texts or how significant they are to understanding our past. That's why one of the goals of this book is to preserve and protect these ancient writings so that they never become lost ever again. I will be breaking down each one of these tablets throughout the course of the book - beginning with *The Myth of Adapa*.

The reason I decided to start with the *Myth of Adapa* is due to how closely it mimics the Gnostic text known as *The Secret Book of John*, which I discussed earlier in the chapter. Notice the strong correlation between these two texts, which provides concrete evidence to show that many of these later stories found within Gnostic, Hebrew and Christian writings were all borrowed from earlier Mesopotamian cuneiform tablets - which often predate them by well over 5,000 years.

The Myth of Adapa tablet 1 states:

> *"He [Adapa] possessed intelligence...*
> *His command like the command of Anu*
> *He [the god Ea] granted him a wide ear to reveal the destiny of the land,*
> *He granted him wisdom but did not grant him eternal life.*
> *In those days, in those years the wise men of Eridu,*
> *Ea had created him as chief among men,*
> *A wise man whose command none shall oppose,*
> *The prudent, the most wise among the Anunnaki was he,*
> *Blameless, of clean hands, anointed, observer of divine statues."*

The Myth of Adapa: British Museum

As most can clearly see, Adapa and Adam are the same being with slightly different names used. This is a common theme that can be seen with certain heroes, gods, and individuals throughout history, such as Atrahasis and Noah. Once one recognizes this pattern, they're able to connect the names used by different cultures to identify the original source of those stories. That's why I hold cuneiform tablets to the highest degree possible and consider them the closest thing we still have to understand the truth of the past. As we go deeper into these texts, I will be including a god name table later in the chapter to aid in understanding the different names used by these deities or beings of antiquity.

Breaking down *The Myth of Adapa* further is begins by stating that a supremely intelligent being - known as Adapa, is created by a god named Ea. This human being is designed in the image of the Anunnaki, but due to his intelligence and perfect nature, he has the potential to become even greater than his creators. Sound familiar?

To the Sumerians, the term "Anunna" translates to mean: "those who from heaven to Earth came", or "those who Anu sent to Earth". While the term Anunnaki is technically Akkadian, it essentially means the same thing. Both terms point to the fact that these creator gods came here from *somewhere* else other than Earth. It doesn't state whether it was from another star system or simply higher dimensions, all we know is that it wasn't from our planet. So then, where did the Anunnaki come from?

Unfortunately, we still do not fully know. Based on the astronomical alignments seen in King and Queen's chambers of the Great Pyramid of Giza, the most likely location to me; based on the little evidence that remains, is from the Orion and Canis Major star constellations. Some of those reading this are undoubtedly going to say: "Nibiru!" but the definition for that term may not accurately portray their place of origin.

Every conclusion that I present to you in this book is based on carefully studying the contents of these ancient texts, as well as evidence from megalithic structures around the world. After all, the most important thing to me is discovering the *truth*.

Further evidence to explain the human origin story can be found in another cuneiform tablet found in the Ashurbanipal Library known as *The Enuma Elish*.

Tablet 6 of **The Enuma Elish** states:

> "They bound him (Kingu), holding him before Ea.
> They inflicted the penalty on him (Kingu) and severed his blood-vessels.
> From his blood he, Ea created mankind,
> On whom he imposed the service of the gods, and set the gods free.
> After the wise Ea had created mankind
> And imposed the service of the gods upon them...
> The task is beyond comprehension.
> The gods were then divided,
> All of the Anunnaki into upper and lower groups,
> He assigned 300 to guard the decrees of Anu and appointed them as guard."

Enuma Elish (British Museum)

The contents of Tablet 6 of the *Enuma Elish* provide further evidence to show that humanity was created in service of the Anunnaki gods here. Notice how it mentions that the Anunnaki were divided in upper and lower groups. This can be equated to higher and lower densities of our reality. That's why the esoteric phrase: "As above so below" is so important to understand when considering their roles in our reality. As the Nag Hammadi states in the chapter *Hypostasis of the Archons*, these beings eventually took on the title of "Rulers of Reality" here. So, who exactly are these Rulers of our Reality?

Anu is considered the divine ruler of this group of deities/gods that call themselves the Anunnaki or Anunna, which is where the name is derived from. For those that are still skeptical, the terms "Anunnaki" and "Anunna" are mentioned more than 50 times across numerous cuneiform tablets, showing that it's not simply an isolated term created by one man, but supported by the world's leading experts. Most of the division that developed withing the Anunnaki over the level of conscious awareness allowed in humanity revolves around Anu's two sons known as Enki (Ea) and Enlil, who were each given dual ownership over our realm.

According to the texts, Enki is credited with the design of Homo sapiens to function as a type of physical laborer here, but ends up falling in love with his creation due to its perfection. Enki's half-brother Enlil becomes increasingly angry and threatened by humanities creative gifts and vows to trap them in endless cycle of chaos and illusion in the third dimensional-physical world. That's why the Secret Book of John states that he is a "jealous god" and "throws Adam (Adapa) into the *lowest* part of the whole material realm."

The reason Enlil did this is because he was given the task by Anu to be the ruler of the physical world and all of mankind. His name provides evidence for that. Breaking down the name Enlil, the letters "En" are masculine for "lord", while "lil" means "air". When you connect them together Enlil's full name means: Lord of the Air. These distinctions of title are very important to distinguish as they help to explain how the events of history unfolded the way that they did.

Meanwhile, Enlil's half-brother Enki; also known as Ea, was tricked into ruling in the underworld, where he was put in charge of balance, knowledge, and even the reincarnation cycles in mankind. That's how he eventually became associated with Osiris in the underworld – known as the Duat, and Ptah in the mortal realm of man. Each of these was a specific role to play in our reality, hence the Gnostic phrase: "Rulers of Reality"

Enki's name breaks down to mean: Lord of the Earth or fresh waters, since "ki" was the ancient name for Earth. Enki has been known by many names throughout history, including Ea, Enkig, Nudimmud, Oannes, or Ninsiku. Similar to Ningishzida (Thoth), Enki has also played many important incarnation roles here as well. Some of the most famous of these incarnations can be seen through the Greek god of Prometheus, the Atlantean king known as Poseidon, the Egyptian god Ptah and the underworld god known as Osiris.

There are numerous texts and cuneiform tablets that explain how these divisions and specific roles were determined, such as *The Legend of Etana* and *Atra-Hasis*, but perhaps the one that is the most famous of all is the Egyptian story of Osiris, Set (Seth), and Horus. The earliest mention of *The Osiris myth* came from what are known as the Pyramid Texts, which are an ancient set of hieroglyphs that were found on the subterranean walls of the pyramids of Teti, Unas, and several of the other pyramids around the Saqqara region of Egypt. These writings were broken up in segments known as Utterance's, which each tell the story of what occurred during that time period. The following translation comes from the South Wall of the Pyramid of Unas.

Utterance 215 states:

You are born for Osiris, o Horus!
You have become more glorious than he,
You have become more powerful than he.
There is no seed of a god which has perished,
neither (has he) who belongs to him.
You will not perish, who belong to him.
Re-Atum does not give you to Osiris, he does not reckon your heart.
Horus, you cannot have power over him, your father cannot have power over him.
You belong, o this one, to this god, as the Twins of Atum said:
"O Osiris, this Unas comes indeed, weary of the Nine, an Imperishable Spirit,
to reckon hearts, to take kas, to grant kas."
Seth, this your brother is here, Osiris, whom has been preserved alive, and who lives that he may punish you!
Cause the Two Lands to bow before this Unas as they bow before Horus!
Cause the Two Lands to fear Unas as they fear Seth!
Be seated before Unas as his god,
open his way in front of the spirits,
that he may stand in front of the spirits like Anubis.
Forward! Forward, before Osiris!
Osiris Unas, take the Eye of Horus, the diminished one, of which Seth has eaten!
You are born for Osiris, o Horus!
You have become more glorious than he,
You have become more powerful than he!

Pyramid texts from Saqqara Egypt

Before the name Egypt ever existed, it was known as the Land of Khem or Khemit. During that time, Enki assumed the role as a powerful pharaoh known as Ptah, before his brother Set (also known as Enlil), betraying and killed him. Thus, forcing Enki to eternally rule in the underworld and take on the role of Osiris. Afterward, Horus; the son of Osiris and Isis, overthrew Set (Seth) to take back control of Egypt and rule as its pharaoh. This allowed Horus to rise up to become a god like his parents.

This story clearly shows the significance that the land of Egypt represented to the Anunnaki. The reason Egypt was so important to them was due to its specific location on the planet - known as geodesy; with a focus on energy ley lines and the 30th parallel of the Earth, which is why the pyramids were built there in the first place. The primary purpose for the pyramids of Egypt was not to be tombs, but act as a type of conduit to balance/harness the electromagnetic energy of the Earth - connecting to a massive set of subterranean chambers below that deal with rejuvenation/death and rebirth cycles here. That's why there was such a focus on the underworld - also called the Duat, in both Egypt and Mesopotamia since eternal life and rejuvenation were the ultimate goals of many of these beings and rulers. However, the technology utilized or means by which these massive pyramids and structures were created is in many ways still a mystery to us today.

Eagle versus the Serpent

Each of these powerful Anunna beings - and the demigods beneath them, took on certain symbols to represent both their mentalities and the specific roles they took on in our reality. Due to the division that developed over time within the Anunna – regarding how humanity should be ruled, empires throughout history became influenced by one side or another, and displayed the associated symbol of that god(s) on their flags and crests.

It's by no means a coincidence that Enlil and his son Ninurta took on the symbol the eagle, since the eagle is the highest-flying bird of all and ruler of the "air". This symbolizes total awareness and domination over our realm, and represents the conquering - war-like nature that came to define them. One cannot help but wonder if this is the reason that so much of human history became focused on war, empire building, and the conquering of other nations. After all, cuneiform tablets and Gnostic writings state that Enlil was specifically assigned to rule over mankind, and - due to jealousy and hatred towards humanity, threatened to keep us in a constant state of chaos and division.

Some would argue that the continuous conflicts seen throughout history in mankind are the result of nothing more than our primitive urges, while others - like myself, believe it has more to do with *preying* on those urges and exploiting them. Remember, if a human being is kept in state of fear, division, and hate, they will always remain in their red-root chakra, which represents their *lowest* state of conscious awareness and vibrational energy.

These various incarnations, names, and titles held by the Anunna can be accurately identified by studying the clues left behind in ancient murals and texts, and then separating out the various traits and symbols that each one of them carried. Quickly, you will notice certain similarities and traits that are consistently shared by these beings in nearly every ancient culture. A good example of this can be found with the Greek god of Zeus (known as Enlil in Sumer), where he's frequently portrayed in statues and murals with an eagle perched near or even on him.

This type of objective reasoning can also be used to identify the specific influences they each had here in the past, by studying the symbolism found in flags and crests around the world. Notice that many of the war-conquering nations of history proudly displayed the eagle on their flags and crests - including the Roman, Spanish, Nazi, and Soviet Empires. It may be quite shocking for many to realize that even the United States eventually adopted the symbol of the eagle as well, even though several of its early founding fathers fiercely opposed that choice and preferring a turkey instead.

In order to better understand the specific roles and incarnations that Enki and Enlil assumed throughout history, I've included a god table below. I would like to strongly point out that evidence exists showing that Enki and Enlil played roles in other cultures as well – such as Hindu and Asian gods; however, I didn't include them in the chart below as that research is ongoing.

Enki and Enlil God Names Table

Human Civilization	Enki	Enlil
Sumerian	Enki	Enlil
Akkadian	Ea	Ellil
Persian	Ahura Mazda	Angra Mainyu
Greek	Prometheus	Zeus
Roman	Neptune	Jupiter
Nordic	Loki	Thor
Slavic	Veles	Perun
Egyptian	Ptah/Osiris	Set/Seth

Even more impressive is that the Anunna are also present in many other ancient texts from around the world where they are referred to as: the Elohim in the Hebrew Bible, the Jinn in Arabian Mythology, the Asuras and Devas in Hindu Mythology, angels and demons on the bible, and countless others.

Out of the thousands of ancient cuneiform tablets that have been recovered in the last several hundred years, the *Atra-Hasis* may be the most significant of them all. This is due to the sheer amount of information it provides regarding the Anunnaki and the human origin story, as well as the violent events that occurred at the end of the last ice age. Before we delve into the actual tablets themselves, I want to provide a little background into who Atrahasis was.

The name Atrahasis means, "exceedingly wise," and was written from the perspective of a past king who ruled over the city of Shuruppak in Sumer, just before the events of the great deluge – 12,000 years ago. Atrahasis was called by many names, including Ziusudra in the Sumerian King List, Utnapishtim in the *Epic of Gilgamesh*, or Noah in the Christian Bible. His father was known as Ubara-Tutu, who was *one* of the last kings of the pre-diluvian cities of Sumer.

This means that they're a vital part of what's known as our Antediluvian or pre-diluvian past (meaning before the flood). This is important because it represents a rare look into the events that occurred during a nearly lost time period in human history - which in many ways is still largely unknown to most of society.

The following translation of the *Atra-Hasis* was done by leading experts in their field - including George Smith and Stephanie Dalley, and should be viewed as highly accurate and credible. Notice the specific terms used here, and carefully ponder the words for yourself to discover their hidden meanings.

Tablet 1 of the *Atra-Hasis* states:

"When the gods instead of man
Did the work, bore the loads,
The gods' load was too great,
The work too hard, the trouble too much.
They took and cast the lots; the gods made the division.
Anu went up to the sky, and Enlil took the earth for his people.
The bolt which bars the sea was assigned to far-sighted Enki.
When Anu had gone up to the sky,
And the gods of the Apsu had gone below,
The Anunnaki of the sky made the Igigi bear the workload.
The Igigi gods had to dig out canals,
Had to clear channels, the lifelines of the land.
For 3,600 years they bore the excess.
Hard work, night and day.
They groaned and blamed each other,
Come, let us carry Enlil,
The counselor of the gods, the warrior, from his dwelling.
And get him to relieve us of our hard work!
Now, cry battle!
Let us mix fight with battle!
The Igigi set fire to their tools,
Put aside their spades for fire.
When they reached the gate of warrior Enlil's dwelling,
It was night, the middle watch,
Ekur was surrounded, Enlil had not realized.
Enlil sent for Anu to be brought down to him,
Enki was fetched into his presence,

Anu, king of the sky was present,
Enki, king of the Apsu attended.
All the great Anunnaki were present.
The Igigi declared,
"Every single one of us declared war!
We have put a stop to the digging.
The load is excessive, it is killing us!
Anu made his voice heard and spoke to the gods his brothers,
"What are we complaining of?
Their work was indeed too hard, their trouble was too much."
Ea made his voice heard and spoke;
"Let us create a mortal man
So that he may bear the yoke, the work of Enlil,
Let man bear the load of the gods."
Nintu made her voice heard, and spoke;
"On the first, seventh, and fifteenth of the month
I shall make a purification by washing.
Then one god should be slaughtered.
Then a god and a man will be mixed together in clay.
Let a ghost come into existence from the god's flesh
And let the ghost exist so as not to forget the slain god."

Atrahasis Tablet (British Museum)

The Anunnaki

According to Tablet 1 of the *Atra-Hasis*, the Anunnaki are part of an ancient group of creator beings or deities that are composed of several different hierarchical subgroups - known as the Igigi or Anunnaki/Anunna. The only problem is that these tablets don't provide much information to explain why these beings came here in the first place, or even where they originally came from. However, there are a few hints hidden in these texts that provide some clues. Let's review what they actually say, and then use logic to connect the dots.

The *Atra-Hasis* and *Enuma Elish* state that the Anunnaki came to Earth to create the infrastructure needed for a new civilization here, which later led to the creation of humanity. However, before these events occurred, there appears to be a period of time when the Anunnaki were in conflict with the forces of chaos and nature relating to the primordial energy of Earth known as Tiamat. For those wondering, cuneiform tablets don't actually state at **all** that the Anunnaki came here for gold, only that they needed the help of the Igigi to build temples and clear river channels in the Tigris and Euphrates for agricultural purposes. However, that doesn't mean that the alchemical and energetic properties associated with gold weren't important though.

Of all the cuneiform tablets, the *Enuma Elish* is one of the most enigmatic and mysterious. It describes how the Anunnaki came to Earth long ago in the past (no reason is given) and got involved in what appears to be some sort of cosmic struggle with a celestial being called Tiamat. The cuneiform texts state that Marduk (the son of Enki) split Tiamat in half – leading to the creation of what we think of as Earth. After years of studying the *Enuma Elish*, and comparing to other Babylonian and Sumerian tablets that mention Tiamat, I believe that the Anunnaki were involved with altering some of the planets in the Solar System and terraforming Earth (Ki) – in order for life to flourish here. But why? Clearly, Earth was very important to them. The fact that the Anunnaki knew these details about our early Solar System means they are truly an ancient race of beings that could be *millions* if not *billions* of years old – who seem to travel between different time periods in history. As impossible as that may sound, I want to provide evidence that supports that conclusion.

As I have previously pointed out, the late Assyriologist George Smith should be considered the *top expert* of cuneiform translation/interpretation in the world. Even though he is no longer alive today, his contributions and translations relating to ancient Mesopotamian history should be held with the highest regard. That's why the conclusions he presents in his book, *The Chaldean Account of Genesis*, are so valuable to understand and ponder. In particular though, is one passage towards the end of the book in which George summarizes his thoughts on the role of Anunnaki here stating:

"Most of the other stories, so far as I can judge, are fixed to the great period before the Flood, when celestial visitors came **backwards** and **forwards** to the earth, and the inhabitants of the world were clearly divided into the good and bad…"

George Smith calls the Anunnaki "celestial visitors" who came to the Earth during different time periods in history and assumed dualistic roles in our reality. This statement also leads one to conclude that the Anunnaki are higher dimensional beings that have the ability to time travel. The important aspect to understand when comparing the conclusions presented by George Smith, along with the information derived in the *Enuma Elish*, is that the Anunnaki played a key role in Earth's history. Whether that was through the means of some kind of terraforming, or ancient magick, there are numerous tablets that discuss the need to conquer the forces of chaos/nature here in order to create a *future* civilization and celestial heaven on earth.

Despite how difficult this concept may be to accept; these ancient texts clearly state that the Anunnaki are sentient beings who are powerful enough to effect entire planets and star systems. That's why we should never underestimate how significant their role was in our story. However, some will undoubtably read the first tablet of the *Enuma Elish* - other cuneiform texts, and come to the false conclusion that the Anunnaki are nothing more than symbolic representations of the forces of nature/celestial bodies and aren't actually literal beings. Allow me to point out some key things that will hopefully help to bring clarity to these tablets' meanings and separate what is literal from symbolic.

The most important thing to understand when reading and deciphering ancient texts from around the world - such as cuneiform tablets, Sanskrit, Mayan Codex's, or Egyptian writings, is that these cultures worshipped *both* literal gods, and the forces of nature/celestial bodies of the Milky Way Galaxy. To make things even more confusing, some of these beings or "gods" decided to represent themselves through celestial bodies and stars. For instance, in the Code of Hammurabi - an ancient Babylonian text, King Hammurabi references both Bel-Marduk and Shamash when he describes his right to rule over the region. When one extensively studies these two terms, they find that Marduk was considered the patron god of Babylon - the first-born son of Enki, while "Shamash" is referencing the solar deity Anu. Either way, they're both real beings - with one connecting back to the Prime Creator or Source. This is why reading and understanding these esoteric texts can be so confusing.

Ever more frustrating is that some of these texts have been *incorrectly* translated by some academics who are often biased towards placing too much value on the forces of nature and celestial representations, rather than literal beings. That's the reason why so many mainstream "experts" are unwilling to accept that the Anunna are real, since it would require *completely* re-writing the human origin story and accepting that sentient life exists in the universe. Someday, however, this will change as ample evidence exists for their influences in ancient civilizations across the planet.

I would like to point out that not only is there extensive evidence for the influences of the Anunnaki on Earth, but also on the Moon and perhaps Mars. For those who don't know, the specific ratio and size of our moon in comparison to the Earth is the *largest* that astronomers have ever observed in the Milky Way Galaxy. Furthermore, between the years of 1972 and 1977, NASA began conducting a series of tests to determine the composition of the moon by shooting rockets onto its surface. Shockingly, they found that "the moon rang like a bell."

So, what exactly does that mean? The fact that the moon is already much larger than normal - per the ratio of Earth, implies that it was likely artificially created and placed there for a *reason*. Secondly, if the moon "rang like a bell", that would provide evidence that it was deliberately hollowed out for either an energetic-density purpose, or perhaps to live inside - maybe both. Irregardless, those anomalies would have been nearly impossible to have been created through natural processes. Therefore, it seems probable to me that the moon plays *some* kind of a role in our story here and with Earth, beyond simply tidal changes and lunar cycles. What exactly that role is we don't fully know yet.

In order to better understand *The Epic of Humanity* – regarding the human origin story and influences of the Anunnaki, let's review the cuneiform tablets of the *Atra-Hasis*.

Tablet 1 of the *Atra-Hasis* starts by stating:

> *"When the gods instead of man*
> *Did the work, bore the loads,*
> *The gods' load was too great,*
> *The work too hard, the trouble too much.*
> *They took and cast the lots; the gods made the division...*
> *When Anu had gone up to the sky,*
> *And the gods of the Apsu had gone below,*
> *The Anunnaki of the sky made the Igigi bear the workload."*

The *Atra-Hasis* explains that the Anunnaki came to Earth to create a new civilization here *before* humans came into existence. However, that task of creating a civilization ended up being more challenging than they anticipated as the lower-class demi-gods (the Igigi) were forced into doing all the physical labor required to maintain this new civilization on Earth – which included agriculture and stone masonry.

Notice how it states that the gods "Cast the lots; made the division, the Anunnaki of the sky made the Igigi bear the workload." This implies that at one time, all of these beings were laboring in our physical reality on Earth. Eventually, a subgroup of these gods - known as the Anunnaki, figured out a way to exist in non-corporeal form, meaning without a body, and assumed different roles within the dimensions of our reality here. As hard as that may be to wrap your head around, let me explain further.

Imagine for a moment that you are an advanced being that's no longer constrained by the limitations of a physical body. Somehow, you've managed to conquer the metaphysical laws of nature and are able to move between different dimensions and time. Consider for a moment what the Egyptian, Hindu, and Gnostic people say about our reality. These ancient cultures state that human beings only observe a small fraction of the overall perspective of reality here – composed of higher and lower dimensions/densities. This information also correlates strikingly well with what the laws of quantum mechanics and super string theory state, which claim that our reality is made up of at *least* 9 different dimensions/densities.

Now you may be wondering: Why would an advanced being want to assume different roles in our reality? And for what purpose? Remember the Hermetic law: "As above so below"? It seems that the Anunnaki became focused on playing different dualistic roles in the higher and lower dimensions of our reality in order to control it somehow. Perhaps it was to try and mimic or even replace the one true "God", also known as the creator of the universe (multiverse) here?

The specific wording used in the *Atra-Hasis* is very important to break down and ponder in order to fully understand these concepts. It says that "The Anunnaki of the sky made the Igigi bear the workload." Notice how it says "the Anunnaki of the *sky*. The term "sky" means upper dimensions or beyond Earth, which implies they were already highly sophisticated before they got here. Hence, the term gods that's often used. This specific term rules out the possibility that they are just advanced human beings, as some have proposed.

Getting back to these certain roles that the Anunna assumed in our reality, referred to as "lots" in the *Atra-Hasis*, it states that the reason they did that was because they wanted to avoid physical labor in our reality. This would imply some kind of an energetic or controlling purpose behind their decision. Perhaps they wanted to utilize Earth's abundant electromagnetic energy for a certain kind of technological purpose, or even for the means of immortality? Could that be the reason why most of the pyramids and ancient megalithic monuments on the planet are found near energetic crossing zones, known as ley lines? Or why we find massive granite sarcophagi in subterranean chambers throughout Egypt that are made of solid rock and seem to have never intended to house a mummified human in the first place? To me, the key must be: energy, rejuvenation and immortality.

Tablet 1 of the *Atra-Hasis* continues by saying:

> *"The Igigi gods had to dig out canals,*
> *Had to clear channels, the lifelines of the land.*

> *For 3,600 years they bore the excess."*

After 3,600 years of grueling labor the Igigi gods revolted and demanded relief from the hard work. The number 3,600 is important to consider, as it later became used as a means to measure time by the Sumerians, which they called a "shar". This is how the long reins shown in the *Sumerian King List* were calculated and recorded. Modern academics often criticize the translations done of the *Sumerian King List*, claiming that human beings could never have lived as long as it states. However, those who study this information know that these ancient kings were part of very specific-royal bloodlines that could be traced directly back to the Anunnaki. Not only that, but the long reins and dating mentioned in the *Sumerian King List* also matches up precisely with the kings list recorded by the Babylonian high-priest known as Berosus. This is one of the reasons the Anunnaki were called "gods" in antiquity was because it seemed they never died and were considered immortal.

The exhausting labor involved with building infrastructure and maintaining our world is well documented in Tablet 1 of the *Atra-Hasis*, where it explains in great detail the grueling work involved with digging out and clearing the silt from the river systems used for agriculture. Records indicate that these events likely occurred more than 50,000 years ago.

But wait a minute...Aren't these stories supposed to be just be myths? When one studies the region known as the Fertile Crescent in Mesopotamia, and the various cities mentioned in these tablets, they find that they exactly line up with real locations in the region that is today referred to as Iraq. For instance, we know that the river channels mentioned that the Igigi had to clear were the Tigris and Euphrates Rivers, which are still very important to agriculture in that part of the world today.

Additionally, there is evidence that these ancient pre-diluvian cities – such as Eridu - located along the Euphrates River, may be a literal mirror of the cosmos, with both the river and city locations created to reflect the constellation and stars of Eridanus, as it flows down from Orion. That's why Eridanus is mentioned in ancient star charts – such as the MUL.APIN, as being called: "river of the cosmos". Additionally, Eridu was the very first city ever created after kingship was lowered by the Anunnaki, with each subsequent city mentioned in the *Sumerian King List* and *Eridu Genesis* being built in specific locations to mirror the stars of Eridanus. Nothing was done by accident it seems...

Quickly, you begin to see that the great trick being played here is convince society that these writings are myths and none of this is connected. Once one learns to decipher the allegorical nature and hidden metaphors present within these tablets, they're able to separate out the specific cities, god names, time periods, and kings who ruled there.

Tablet 1 of the *Atra-Hasis* continues by saying

> *"Come, let us carry Enlil,*
> *The counselor of the gods, the warrior, from his dwelling.*

> *And get him to relieve us of our hard work!*
> *Now, cry battle!*
> *The Igigi set fire to their tools,*
> *Put aside their spades for fire.*
> *When they reached the gate of warrior Enlil's dwelling,*
> *It was night, the middle watch,*
> *Ekur was surrounded, Enlil had not realized."*

The name "Ekur" mentioned in the *Atra-Hasis* means "mountain house" and was referring to an ancient mountain temple dedicated to the god Enlil in the city of Nippur, Iraq. In fact, the ruins of that city can still be seen today. On top of that, Eridu - which is mentioned in the *Myth of Adapa, Sumerian King List*, and *Eridu Genesis* tablets as being the first city ever created, is likely the location of the Biblical "Eden". That's why I put so much emphasis on studying these cuneiform tablets, since they allow us a rare glimpse into the past to understand our origins and the historical locations that shaped our story.

The *Atra-Hasis* states that the Igigi eventually decided to revolt from the increasingly difficult, manual labor they had to perform. They grouped up together and decided to storm their leader Enlil's temple in order for him to "relieve" them of the grueling work. This is where the human origin story begins.

Tablet 1 of the *Atra-Hasis* continues by saying:

> *"Anu made his voice heard and spoke to the gods his brothers,*
> *"What are we complaining of?*
> *Their work was indeed too hard, their trouble was too much."*
> *Ea made his voice heard and spoke;*

> *"Let us create a mortal man*
> *So that he may bear the yoke, the work of Enlil,*
> *Let man bear the load of the gods."*
> *Nintu made her voice heard, and spoke;*
> *"On the first, seventh, and fifteenth of the month*
> *I shall make a purification by washing.*
> *Then one god should be slaughtered.*
> *Then a god and a man will be mixed together in clay.*
> *Let a ghost come into existence from the god's flesh*
> *And let the ghost exist so as not to forget the slain god."*

Tablet 1 of the *Atra-Hasis* provides some of the most detailed information we have for the true origin story of mankind, as well as the identity of who these "gods of the Apsu" really were. Before I break this quote down, I would like to point out that the information in the *Atra-Hasis* describing humanities origin story is nearly *identical* to what is said in **Tablet 6** of the Enuma Elish, which states:

> *"They bound him, holding him before Ea.*
> *They inflicted the penalty on him (Kingu) and*
> *severed his (Kingu's) blood-vessels.*
> *From his blood, he, Ea created mankind,*
> *On whom he imposed the service of the gods,*
> *and set the gods free.*
> *After the wise Ea had created mankind*
> *and had imposed the service of the gods upon them,*
> *the task was beyond comprehension.*
> *The gods were then divided,*

> *All of the Anunnaki into upper and lower groups.*
> *He assigned 300 in the heavens to*
> *guard the decrees of Anu, and*
> *appointed them as guard."*

Even after reading these tablets *hundreds* of times, the profound information they provide never ceases to amaze me. I am always struck by the specific way that they chose to convey information, which is often written through the use of specific symbolism and challenging metaphors. It was as if they wanted the true story behind these texts to only be understood by those who could decipher their hidden meanings. Perhaps that is one of the reasons why they remain so unknown and mysterious today. Let's break down this section of the *Atra-Hasis* and *Enuma Elish* together.

Tablet 1 of the *Atra-Hasis* and **Tablet 6** of the Enuma Elish explain that after the Igigi decide to revolt from the manual labor needed on the planet, the Anunnaki council convenes together to decide on a plan. Notice how quickly Ea (Enki) speaks up with his idea of creating mankind. This implies that his decision to create another sentient being was likely predetermined. The reason that is important is because it provides evidence to explain why he - and some of the other Anunna gods, fell in love with their creation. This would eventually lead to a significant rift among the Anunnaki over how advanced this "laborer of the gods" should be - both on a conscious and energetic level, and create the great struggle I frequently refer to as: "The eagle versus the serpent". For this interested in learning more, this topic was more extensively covered in my previous book: *The Stage of Time*.

The *Atra-Hasis* and *Enuma Elish* clay tablets help to explain the reason why scientists find non-coding DNA in human beings that doesn't match *any* other species on the planet, as well as why there is a missing link in the evolutionary timeline of Homo sapiens. Notice at the end of the tablet when the term "ghost" is used to reference the development of consciousness and a soul within the physical body. The real question is: Where did this "non-coding" DNA come from?

This leads us back to the cuneiform tablet known as *The Myth of Adapa*, which I shared and briefly discussed earlier in the chapter. What makes this ancient text so important is that it contains specific wording that provides valuable clues to expand on what is said in both the *Atra-Hasis* and *Enuma Elish*. Recapping briefly, *The Myth of Adapa* states:

"Ea had created him (Adapa –the perfect human) as chief among men,

A wise man whose command none shall oppose,

The prudent, the most wise *among* the **Anunnaki** was he".

Pay close attention to the specific language that's used in the last line. It states that Adapa was: "*The most wise among the Anunnaki*". This provides evidence to show that Homo sapiens are not only closely related to the Anunnaki, but **are** the Anunnaki. After all, one of the Igigi/Anunnaki gods known as Kingu was sacrificed in order to create mankind. That means instead of highly evolved apes fighting over dwindling resources, humanity is designed in the image of perfection to become powerful creator gods - just like the Anunnaki. This information can be quite shocking for many to discover, due to the simplistic and antiquated means by why which most mainstream academics have painted the human origin story. The real question is: Who exactly were the Igigi?

According to cuneiform records, the Igigi were the non-royal demigods of the Anunnaki, who acted as a type of servant or emissary for them. The *Atra-Hasis* states that the Igigi labored on Earth for thousands of years, clearing river channels and building structures, until eventually they revolted and demanded relief from the hard work. That's why the decision was made to create humans in the first place - to fulfill the role of the Igigi here.

Mesopotamian tablets state that the Anunna are governed by a largely male-dominated hierarchy kingship structure, which was directly based on specific royal bloodlines ruling over the rest of society. Sound familiar? That's why "kingship" is mentioned so frequently in many of these ancient texts; such as the *Sumerian King List* and *Legend of Etana*, since it represents the specific model that was chosen for human civilizations to be governed by here. After thousands of years of royal kings and queens ruling in this hierarchy-pyramid structure, it's clear that this model is still largely in place even today. Try not to be fooled by the illusion of an open and free democracy, and instead see the bigger picture for who is *really* in charge of our reality.

When I look around the world at the unbalanced mentalities and fear-based systems that govern most people's lives, I find myself both angry and sad over how humanity has been treated. I don't see this flawed structure and false identity as merely the result of a few powerful families or corrupted secret societies, but a much deeper ideology that connects all the way back to this original kingship model. It's clear to me that an elaborate and highly complex system was eventually created here to turn society into obedient - productive workers that are ruled by fear and ask very few questions to challenge authority.

Remember, the most effective ways to rule over a society is through fear and re-writing their history, while at the same time, promoting war, division, and materialism as the main focus. This "conditioning" of reality was done for the means of trapping humanity in an endless cycle of reincarnation, where they often repeat the same life over and over again until they can finally wake up to the truth.

In the end, humanity's true purpose in life is to grow on a spiritual and physical level - through the means of exploring self-expression and duality, in order to better understand their role in the universe. Whether that means being governed by the higher knowledge and light of truth, or the deception and emptiness of darkness, we are each here to choose which path we'll take based on the law of free will. The ultimate question is: Which path will humanity choose?

Chapter 3 – The Founders of Atlantis

By Billy Carson

The ancient texts mentioned below are among the most significant and influential in human history, each originating from different cultures and offering profound insights into their respective civilizations. All while drawing inspiration and influence from one another. The beings written about in many ancient texts discovered all over the world are quite possibly the founders of the Atlantean civilization. The name Anunnaki is merely a title for any being that comes from heaven to Earth. The civilization that they built was an interplanetary civilization known as Atlantis.

This chapter explores the fascinating and speculative hypothesis that the gods depicted in ancient texts like the Mahabharata, Bhagavad Gita, Indian Vedas, Egyptian Book of the Dead, Tibetan Book of the Dead, and Sumerian Tablets might be Anunnaki, an ancient group of deities in Mesopotamian mythology. These texts, each a cornerstone of its respective culture, offer rich narratives and teachings that have shaped religious and philosophical thought throughout history. They may be the gods that created the Atlantean civilization.

Summary of Ancient Texts:

1. Mahabharata: An epic narrative of the Kurukshetra War and the fates of the Kaurava and the Pandava princes. The Mahabharata is one of the two major Sanskrit epics of ancient India. It encompasses an array of philosophical and devotional material, such as a discussion of the four "goals of life." Its diverse content makes it more than just a story; it represents the Indian ethos itself.

Excerpt from the Mahabharata:

> THE MAHABHARATA
> BHISHMA PARVA
> SECTION I
> (Jamvu-khanda Nirmana Parva)
> OM! HAVING BOWED down to Narayana, and Nara, the most exalted of male beings, and also to the goddess Saraswati, must the word 'Jaya' be uttered.
> Janamejaya said,--"How did those heroes, the Kurus, the Pandavas, and the Somakas, and the high-souled kings assembled together from various countries, fight?"
> Vaisampayana said,--"Listen thou, O lord of the earth, how those heroes,--the Kurus, the Pandavas, and the Somakas,--fought on the sacred plain of the Kurukshetra. 1 Entering Kurukshetra, the Pandavas endued with great might, along with the Somakas, advanced, desirous of victory, against the Kauravas. Accomplished in the study of the Vedas, all (of them) took great delight in battle. Expectant of success in battle, with their troops (they) faced the fight. Approaching the army of

Dhritarashtra's son, those (warriors) invincible in battle 2 stationed themselves with their troops on the western part (of the plain), their faces turned towards the east. Yudhishthira, the son of Kunti, caused tents by thousands to be set up according to rule, beyond the region called Samantapanchaka. The whole earth seemed then to be empty, divested of horses and men, destitute of cars and elephants, and with only the children and the old left (at home). From the whole area of Jamvudwipa over which the sun sheds his rays, 3 was collected that force, O best of kings. Men of all races, 4 assembled together, occupied an area extending for many Yojanas over districts, rivers, hills, and woods. That bull among men, king Yudhishthira, ordered excellent food and other articles of enjoyment for all of them along with their animals. And Yudhishthira fixed diverse watch-words for them; so that one saying this should be known as belonging to the Pandavas. And that descendant of Kuru's race also settled names and badges for all of them for recognition during time of battle.

"Beholding the standard-top of Pritha's son, the high-souled son of

p. 2

[paragraph continues] Dhritarashtra, with a white umbrella held over his head, in the midst of a thousand elephants, and surrounded by his century of brothers, began with all the kings (on his side) to array his troops against the son of Pandu. Seeing Duryodhana, the Panchalas who took delight in battle, were filled with joy and blew their loud-sounding conches and cymbals of sweet sounds. Beholding those troops so delighted, Pandu's son and Vasudeva of great energy had their hearts filled with joy. And those tigers among men, Vasudeva and Dhananjaya, seated on one car, having felt great joy, both blew their celestial conches. And hearing the blare of Gigantea and the loud blast of Theodotes belonging unto the two, the combatants ejected urine and excreta. As other animals are filled with fear on hearing the voice of the roaring lion, even so became that force upon hearing those blasts. A frightful dust arose and nothing could be seen, for the sun himself, suddenly enveloped by it, seemed to have set. 1 A black cloud poured a shower of flesh and blood over the troops all around. All this seemed extraordinary. A wind rose there, bearing along the earth myriads of stony nodules, and afflicting therewith the combatants by hundreds and thousands. (For all that), O monarch, both armies, filled with joy, stood addrest for battle, on Kurukshetra like two agitated oceans. Indeed, that encounter of the two armies was highly wonderful, like that of two oceans when the end of the Yuga is arrived. The whole earth was empty, having only the children and the old left (at home), in consequence of that large army mustered by the Kauravas. 2 Then the Kurus, the Pandavas, and the Somakas made certain covenants, and settled the rules, O bull of Bharata's race, regarding the different kinds of combat. Persons equally circumstanced must encounter each other, fighting fairly. And if having fought fairly the combatants withdraw (without fear of molestation), even that would be gratifying to us. Those who engaged in contests of words should be fought against with words. Those that left the ranks should never be slain. 3 A car-warrior should have a car-warrior for his antagonist; he on the neck of an elephant should have a similar combatant for his foe; a horse should be met by a horse, and a foot-soldier, O Bharata; should be met by a foot-soldier. Guided by considerations of fitness, willingness, daring and might, one should strike another, giving notice. No one should strike another that is unprepared 4 or panic-struck. One engaged with another, one seeking quarter, one retreating, one whose weapon is rendered unfit, uncased in mail, should never be struck. Car-drivers, animals (yoked to cars or carrying weapons) men

p. 3

engaged in the transport of weapons, 1 players on drums and blowers of conches should never be struck. Having made these covenants, the Kurus, and the Pandavas, and the Somakas wondered much, gazing at each other. And having stationed (their forces thus), those bulls among men, those high-souled ones, with their troops, became glad at heart, their joy being reflected on their countenances."

Mahabharata: Wikipedia

2. Bhagavad Gita: Often considered a part of the Mahabharata, this 700-verse Hindu scripture is a conversation between Prince Arjuna and the god Krishna, who serves as his charioteer. This sacred text is a philosophical and spiritual classic that discusses important concepts like duty, righteousness, and the nature of reality. Who are Krishna and Arjuna in The Bhagavad Gita? Why are they so important to the story?

Krishna and Arjuna in The Bhagavad Gita have an important connection. Arjuna, a prince is deeply conflicted about a battle, and Krishna, a god, helps him understand important lessons about himself and his spirituality.

Excerpt from the Bhagavad Gita:

> Prince Arjuna leads the Pandavas' army. His chariot is driven by Sri Krishna, an incarnation of the god Vishnu, who has taken a mortal form in The Bhagavad Gita. Krishna has been Arjuna's friend and advisor throughout his life, but he can't fight this battle. Leading the army is Arjuna's dharma—his duty and destiny. Krishna is only there to support him.
> (Shortform note: "Sri," sometimes spelled "Shri," is a term of respect that doesn't have a direct translation.)
> As Arjuna sees that the fighting's about to start, he asks Krishna to drive his chariot in between the two armies so that he can take a closer look at his enemies. When he sees the people in the Kauravas' army, he recognizes many of them as his own family and friends.
> Arjuna is overcome with despair. He tells Krishna that he doesn't want to fight against his own family, and that his family fighting within itself will lead to chaos in the kingdom. He also says that there are great heroes and respected scholars on the other side, and Arjuna questions how he could ever live with himself if he killed them in battle. Arjuna says that it would be better to lay down his weapons and let the Kauravas kill him.
> Krishna replies that, though Arjuna is speaking from the heart, he is also speaking from ignorance. Although physical bodies can be destroyed, a person's essence will be reborn again and again, unchanged, through the process of reincarnation. Therefore, Arjuna wouldn't be killing anybody, and there would be no reason to grieve for them. This is an important

> conversation between Krishna and Arjuna in The Bhagavad Gita.
>
> Krishna compares reincarnation to the changes that a person goes through over a single lifetime, from childhood to adulthood to old age. You wouldn't say that a person became someone else after growing up, and in the same sense, you shouldn't think of someone who's been reincarnated as becoming a different person.

Bhagavad Gita: Wikipedia

3. Indian Vedas: These are a large body of religious texts originating in ancient India. Composed in Vedic Sanskrit, the texts constitute the oldest layer of Sanskrit literature and the oldest scriptures of Hinduism. They are a collection of hymns and other religious texts composed over several centuries, beginning in the second millennium BCE.

There are four Vedas, the Rig Veda, Sama Veda, Yajur Veda and Atharva Veda. The Vedas are the primary texts of Hinduism. They also had a vast influence on Buddhism, Jainism, and Sikhism. Traditionally the text of the Vedas was coeval with the universe. Scholars have determined that the Rig Veda, the oldest of the four Vedas, was composed about 1500 B.C., and codified about 600 B.C. It is unknown when it was finally committed to writing, but this probably was at some point after 300 B.C.

Excerpt from the Indian Vedas:

> HYMN I. Agni.
> 1 I Laud Agni, the chosen Priest, God, minister of sacrifice,
> The hotar, lavishest of wealth.
> 2 Worthy is Agni to be praised by living as by ancient seers.
> He shall bring hitherward the Gods.
> 3 Through Agni man obtaineth wealth, yea, plenty waxing day by day,
> Most rich in heroes, glorious.
> 4 Agni, the perfect sacrifice which thou encompassest about
> Verily goeth to the Gods.
> 5 May Agni, sapient-minded Priest, truthful, most gloriously great,
> The God, come hither with the Gods.
> 6 Whatever blessing, Agni, thou wilt grant unto thy worshipper,
> That, A giras, is indeed thy truth.
> 7 To thee, dispeller of the night, O Agni, day by day with prayer
> Bringing thee reverence, we come
> 8 Ruler of sacrifices, guard of Law eternal, radiant One,
> Increasing in thine own abode.
> 9 Be to us easy of approach, even as a father to his son:
> Agni, be with us for our weal.

Indian Vedas: Wikipedia

4. Egyptian Book of the Dead: An ancient Egyptian funerary text, the Book of the Dead was used from the beginning of the New Kingdom (around 1550 BCE) to around 50 BCE. It's a collection of spells, prayers, and incantations designed to guide the deceased through the dangers of the underworld, ultimately leading to a life of eternity.

THE LEGEND OF OSIRIS.

The main features of the Egyptian religion constant.

The chief features of the Egyptian religion remained unchanged from the Vth and VIth dynasties down to the period when the Egyptians embraced Christianity, after the preaching of St. Mark the Apostle in Alexandria, A.D. 69, so firmly had the early beliefs taken possession of the Egyptian mind; and the Christians in Egypt, or Copts as they are commonly called, the racial descendants of the ancient Egyptians, seem never to have succeeded in divesting themselves of the superstitious and weird mythological conceptions which they inherited from their heathen ancestors. It is not necessary here to repeat the proofs, of this fact which M. Amélineau has brought together,[1] or to adduce evidence from the lives of the saints, martyrs and ascetics; but it is of interest to note in passing that the translators of the New Testament into Coptic rendered the Greek {Greek a!'dhs} by ###, amenti, the name which the ancient Egyptians gave to the abode of man after death,[3] and that the Copts peopled it with beings whose prototypes are found on the ancient monuments.

Persistence of the legend of Osiris and the belief in the resurrection.

The chief gods mentioned in the pyramid texts are identical with those whose names are given on tomb, coffin and papyrus in the latest dynasties; and if the names of the great cosmic gods, such as Ptah and Khnemu, are of rare occurrence, it should be remembered that the gods of the dead must naturally occupy the chief place in this literature which concerns the dead. Furthermore, we find that the doctrine of eternal life and of the resurrection of a glorified or transformed body, based upon the ancient story of the resurrection of Osiris after a cruel death and horrible mutilation, inflicted by the powers of evil, was the same in all periods, and that the legends of the most ancient times were accepted without material alteration or addition in the texts of the later dynasties.

Excerpts from the Egyptian Book Of The Dead:

> **Hymn to Osiris.**
> "(1) Hail to thee, Osiris, lord of eternity, king of the gods, thou who hast many names, thou disposer of created things, thou who hast hidden forms in the temples, thou sacred one, thou KA who dwellest in Tattu, thou mighty (2) one in Sekhem, thou lord to whom invocations are made in Anti, thou who art over the offerings in Annu, thou lord who makest inquisition in two-fold right and truth, thou hidden soul, the lord of Qerert, thou who disposest affairs in the city of the White Wall, thou soul of Ra, thou very body of Ra who restest in (3) Suten-henen, thou to whom adorations are made in the region of Nart, thou who makest the soul to rise, thou lord of the Great House in Khemennu, thou mighty of terror in Shas-hetep, thou lord of eternity, thou chief of Abtu, thou who sittest upon thy throne in Ta-tchesert, thou whose name is established in the mouths of (4) men, thou unformed matter of the world, thou god Tum, thou who providest with food the ka's who are with the company of the gods, thou perfect khu among khu's, thou provider of the waters of Nu, thou giver of the wind, thou producer of the wind of the evening from thy nostrils for the satisfaction of thy heart. Thou makest (5) plants to grow at thy desire, thou givest birth to . . . . ; to thee are obedient the stars in the heights, and thou openest the mighty gates. Thou art the lord to whom hymns of praise are sung in the southern heaven, and unto thee are adorations paid in the northern heaven. The never setting stars (6) are before thy face, and they are thy thrones, even as

also are those that never rest. An offering cometh to thee by the command of Seb. The company of the gods adoreth thee, the stars of the tuat bow to the earth in adoration before thee, [all] domains pay homage to thee, and the ends of the earth offer entreaty and supplication. When those who are among the holy ones (7) see thee they tremble at thee, and the whole world giveth praise unto thee when it meeteth thy majesty. Thou art a glorious sahu among the sahu's, upon thee hath dignity been conferred, thy dominion is eternal, O thou beautiful Form of the company of the gods; thou gracious one who art beloved by him that (8) seeth thee. Thou settest thy fear in all the world, and through love for thee all proclaim thy name before that of all other gods. Unto thee are offerings made by all mankind, O thou lord to whom commemorations are made, both in heaven and in earth. Many are the shouts of joy that rise to thee at the Uak[*] festival, and cries of delight ascend to thee from the (9) whole world with one voice. Thou art the chief and prince of thy brethren, thou art the prince of the company of the gods, thou stablishest right and truth everywhere, thou placest thy son upon thy throne, thou art the object of praise of thy father Seb, and of the love of thy mother Nut. Thou art exceeding mighty, thou overthrowest those who oppose thee, thou art mighty of hand, and thou slaughterest thine (10) enemy. Thou settest thy fear in thy foe, thou removest his boundaries, thy heart is fixed, and thy feet are watchful. Thou art the heir of Seb and the sovereign of all the earth;

[* This festival took place on the 17th and 18th days of the month Thoth; see Brugsch, Kalendarische Inschriften, p. 235.] {footnote page liii}

Seb hath seen thy glorious power, and hath commanded thee to direct the (11) universe for ever and ever by thy hand.

"Thou hast made this earth by thy hand, and the waters thereof, and the wind thereof, the herb thereof, all the cattle thereof, all the winged fowl thereof, all the fish thereof, all the creeping things thereof, and all the four-footed beasts thereof. (12) O thou son of Nut, the whole world is gratified when thou ascendest thy father's throne like Ra. Thou shinest in the horizon, thou sendest forth thy light into the darkness, thou makest the darkness light with thy double plume, and thou floodest the world with light like the (13) Disk at break of day. Thy diadem pierceth heaven and becometh a brother unto the stars, O thou form of every god. Thou art gracious in command and in speech, thou art the favoured one of the great company of the gods, and thou art the greatly beloved one of the lesser company of the gods.

"Thy sister put forth her protecting power for thee, she scattered abroad those who were her enemies, (14) she drove back evil hap, she pronounced mighty words of power, she made cunning her tongue, and her words failed not. The glorious Isis was perfect in command and in speech, and she avenged her brother. She sought him without ceasing, (15) she wandered round and round the earth uttering cries of pain, and she rested[*] not until she had found him. She overshadowed him with her feathers, she made wind with her wings, and she uttered cries at the burial of her brother. (16) She raised up the prostrate form of him whose heart was still, she took from. him of his essence, she conceived and brought forth a child,[+] she suckled it in secret (?) and none knew the place thereof; and the arm of the child hath waxed strong in the great house of Seb. (17) The company of the gods rejoiceth and is glad at the coming of Osiris's son Horus, and firm of heart and triumphant is the son of Isis, the heir of Osiris."[++]

[*. Literally, "she alighted not,"; the whole passage here justifies Plutarch's statement (De Iside Osiride, 16) concerning Isis: {Greek Au?th`n de` genome'nhn xelido'na tu~j ki'oni peripi'tesðai kai` ðrhnei~n}.

+. Compare Plutarch, op. cit., §19: {Greek T`hn d' I?'sin th`n teleuth`n e`ks O?si'ridos suggenome'nou tekei~n h?li'to'mhnon kai` a?sðenh~ toi~s ka'twðen gui'ois to`n A?rpokra'thn}.
++. The remainder of the hymn refers to Horus.]]
{p. liii}

Egyptian Book of the Dead: Wikipedia

5. Tibetan Book of the Dead: Known in Tibetan as "Bardo Thodol," this text is a guide for the deceased during the state that intervenes between death and the next rebirth. It is a key work of Tibetan Buddhism, reflecting its comprehensive perspective on life, death, and rebirth.

Excerpts from the Tibetan Book Of The Dead:

> **Part I: The Primary Clear Light Seen At the Moment of Ego-Loss.**
> All individuals who have received the practical teachings of this manual will, if the text be remembered, be set face to face with the ecstatic radiance and will win illumination instantaneously, without entering upon hallucinatory struggles and without

further suffering on the age-long pathway of normal evolution which traverses the various worlds of game existence.

This doctrine underlies the whole of the Tibetan model. Faith is the first step on the "Secret Pathway." Then comes illumination and with it certainty; and when the goal is won, emancipation. Success implies very unusual preparation in consciousness expansion, as well as much calm, compassionate game playing (good karma) on the part of the participant. If the participant can be made to see and to grasp the idea of the empty mind as soon as the guide reveals it - that is to say, if he has the power to die consciously - and, at the supreme moment of quitting the ego, can recognize the ecstasy which will dawn upon him then, and become one with it, all game bonds of illusion are broken asunder immediately: the dreamer is awakened into reality simultaneously with the mighty achievement of recognition.

It is best if the guru (spiritual teacher), from whom the participant received guiding instructions, is present, but if the guru cannot be present, then another experienced person; or it the latter is also unavailable, then a person whom the participant trusts should be available to read this manual without imposing any of his own games. Thereby the participant will be put in mind of what he had previously heard of the experience and will at once come to recognize the fundamental Light and undoubtedly obtain liberation.

Liberation is the nervous system devoid of mental-conceptual activity. [Realization of the Voidness, the Unbecome, the Unborn, the Unmade, the Unformed, implies Buddhahood, Perfect Enlightenment - the state of the divine mind of the Buddha. It may be helpful to remember that this ancient doctrine is not in conflict with modern physics. The theoretical physicist and cosmologist, George Gamow, presented in 1950 a viewpoint which is close to the phenomenological experience described by the Tibetan lamas.

If we imagine history running back in time, we inevitably come to the epoch of the "big squeeze" with all the galaxies, stars, atoms and atomic nuclei squeezed, so to speak, to a pulp. During that early stage of evolution, matter must have been dissociated into its elementary components.... We call this primordial mixture ylem.

At this first point in the evolution of the present cycle, according to this first-rank physicist, there existed only the Unbecome, the Unborn, the Unformed. And this, according to astrophysicists, is the way it will end; the silent unity of the Unformed. The Tibetan Buddhists suggest that the uncluttered intellect can experience what astrophysics confirms. The Buddha Vairochana, the Dhyani Buddha of the Center, Manifester of Phenomena, is the highest path to enlightenment. As the source of all organic life, in him all things visible and invisible have their consummation and absorption. He is associated with the Central Realm of the Densely-Packed, i.e., the seed of all universal forces and things are densely packed together. This remarkable convergence of modern astrophysics and ancient lamaism demands no complicated explanation. The cosmological awareness- and awareness of every other natural process- is there in the cortex. You can confirm this preconceptual mystical knowledge by empirical observation and measurement, but it's all there inside your skull. Your neurons "know" because they are linked directly to the process, are part of it.] The mind in its conditioned state, that is to say, when limited to words and ego games, is continuously in thought-formation activity. The nervous system in a state of quiescence, alert, awake but not active is comparable to what Buddhists call the highest state of dhyana (deep meditation) when still united to a human body. The conscious recognition of the Clear Light induces an ecstatic condition of consciousness such as saints and mystics of the West have called illumination.

The first sign is the glimpsing of the "Clear Light of Reality," "the infallible mind of the pure mystic state." This is the awareness of energy transformations with no imposition of mental categories.

The duration of this state varies with the individual. It depends upon experience, security, trust, preparation and the surroundings. In those who have had even a little practical experience of the tranquil state of non-game awareness, and in those who have happy games, this state can last from thirty minutes to several hours.

In this state, realization of what mystics call the "Ultimate Truth" is possible, provided that sufficient preparation has been made by the person beforehand. Otherwise he cannot benefit now, and must wander on into lower and lower conditions of hallucinations, as determined by his past games, until he drops back to routine reality.

Tibetan Book of the Dead: Wilipedia

6. Sumerian Tablets: These ancient texts, written in the Sumerian language on clay tablets, provide a fascinating view into the world's oldest known form of writing. They contain a variety of records, such as myths, hymns, laws, and treaties, offering a window into the daily lives and beliefs of one of the world's earliest civilizations.

Excerpts from the Epic Of Atrahasis:

> The conditions immediately after the Creation: the Lower Gods have to work very hard and start to complain
> Revolt of the Lower Gods
> Negotiations with the Great Gods
> Proposal to create humans, to relieve the Lower Gods from their labor
> Creation of the Man
> Man's noisy behavior; new complaints from the gods
> The supreme god Enlil's decision to extinguish mankind by a Great Flood
> Atrahasis is warned in a dream
> Enki explains the dream to Atra asis (and betrays the plan)
> Construction of the Ark
> Boarding of the Ark
> Departure

The Great Flood
The gods are hungry because there are no farmers left to bring sacrifices, and decide to spare Atra asis, even though he is a rebel
Regulations to cut down the noise: childbirth, infant mortality, and celibacy
Complaints of the Lower Gods
[1] When the gods were man
they did forced labor, they bore drudgery.
Great indeed was the drudgery of the gods,
the forced labor was heavy, the misery too much:

[5] the seven great Anunna-gods were burdening
the Igigi-godsnote with forced labor.

[Lacuna]

[21] The gods were digging watercourses,
canals they opened, the life of the land.
The Igigi-gods were digging watercourses
canals they opened, the life of the land.

[25] The Igigi-gods dug the Tigris river
and the Euphrates thereafter.
Springs they opened from the depths,
wells ... they established.
...
They heaped up all the mountains.

[Several lines missing]
[34] ... years of drudgery.
[35] ... the vast marsh.
They counted years of drudgery,
... and forty years, too much!

... forced labor they bore night and day.
They were complaining, denouncing,
[40] muttering down in the ditch:
"Let us face up to our foreman the prefect,
he must take off our heavy burden upon us!
Enlil, counsellor of the gods, the warrior,
come, let us remove him from his dwelling;

[45] Enlil, counsellor of the gods, the warrior,
come, let us remove him from his dwelling!"

[Several lines missing]

[61] "Now them, call for battle,
battle let us join, warfare!"
The gods heard his words:
they set fire to their tools,
[65] they put fire to their spaces,
and flame to their workbaskets.
Off they went, one and all,
to the gate of the warrior Enlil's abode.
...
Insurrection of the Lower Gods
[70] It was night, half-way through the watch,
the house was surrounded, but the god did not know.
It was night, half-way through the watch,
Ekur was surrounded, but Enlil did not know!
[Several lines missing; the great gods send a messenger]
The Great Gods Send a Messenger
[132] Nusku opened his gate,
took his weapons and went ... Enlil.
In the assembly of all the gods,

[135] he knelt, stood up, expounded the command,

"Anu, your father,
your counsellor, the warrior Enlil,
your prefect, Ninurta,
and your bailiff Ennugi have sent me to say:
[140] 'Who is the instigator of this battle?
Who is the instigator of these hostilities?
Who declared war,
that battle has run up to the gate of Enlil?
In ...
[145] he transgressed the command of Enlil.'"

Reply by the Lower Gods
"Everyone of us gods has declared war;
...
We have set ... un the excvation,
excessive drudgery has killed us,

[150] our forced labor was heavy, the misery too much!
Now, everyone of us gods
has resolved on a reckoning with Enlil."
[The great gods decide to create man, to relieve the lower gods from their misery.]
Proposals by Ea, Belet-ili, and Enki
[a1] Ea made ready to speak,
and said to the gods, his brothers:
"What calumny do we lay to their charge?
Their forced labor was heavy, their misery too much!
[a5] Every day ...
the outcry was loud, we could hear the clamor.
There is ...
Belet-ili, the midwife, is present.note
Let her create, then, a human, a man,

[a10] Let him bear the yoke!

Let him bear the yoke!
Let man assume the drudgery of the god."
Belet-ili, the midwife, is present.

[190] Let the midwife create a human being!
Let man assume the drudgery of the god."
They summoned and asked the goddess
the midwife of the gods, wise Mami:note
"Will you be the birth goddess, creatress of mankind?

[195] Create a human being, that he bear the yoke,
let him bear the yoke, the task of Enlil,
let man assume the drudgery of the god."
Nintu made ready to speak,note
and said to the great gods:

[200] "It is not for me to do it,
the task is Enki's.
He it is that cleanses all,
let him provide me the clay so I can do the making."
Enki made ready to speak,

[205] and said to the great gods:
"On the first, seventh, and fifteenth days of the month,
let me establish a purification, a bath.
Let one god be slaughtered,
then let the gods be cleansed by immersion.

[210] Let Nintu mix clay with his flesh and blood.
Let that same god and man be thoroughly mixed in the clay.
Let us hear the drum for the rest of the time.

[215] From the flesh of the god let a spirit remain,
let it make the living know its sign,

lest he be allowed to be forgotten, let the spirit remain."
The great Anunna-gods, who administer destinies,

[220] answered "yes!" in the assembly.

The Creation of Man
On the first, seventh, and fifteenth days of the month, note
he established a purification, a bath.
They slaughtered Aw-ilu, who had the inspiration, in their assembly.

[225] Nintu mixed clay with his flesh and blood.
That same god and man were thoroughly mixed in the clay.
For the rest of the time they would hear the drum.
From the flesh of the god the spirit remained.
It would make the living know its sign.

[230] Lest he be allowed to be forgotten, the spirit remained.
After she had mixed the clay,
she summoned the Anunna, the great gods.
The Igigi, the great gods, spat upon the clay.

[235] Mami made rady to speak,
and said to the great gods:
"You ordered me the task and I have completed it!
You have slaughtered the god, along with his inspiration.

[240] I have done away with your heavy forced labor,
I have imposed your drudgery on man.
You have bestowed clamor upon mankind.
I have released the yoke, I have made restoration."
They heard this speech of hers,

[245] they ran, free of care, and kissed her feet, saying:

"Formerly we used to call you Mami,
now let your name be Belet-kala-ili:"note
[The human population increases and their noise disturbs the gods, who decide to wipe out mankind. The god Enki, however, sends a dream to Atrahasis. When the text resumes, Enki is still speaking.]

Enki explains Atrahasis' dream
[i.b35] "Enlil committed an evil deed against the people."

[i.c11] Atrahasis made ready to speak,
and said to his lord:
"Make me know the meaning of the dream.
let me know, that I may look out for its consequence."

[i.c15] Enki made ready to speak,
and said to his servant:
"You might say, 'Am I to be looking out while in the bedroom?'
Do you pay attention to message that I speak for your:

[i.c20] 'Wall, listen to me!
Reed wall, pay attention to all my words!
Flee the house, build a boat,
forsake possessions, and save life.

[i.c25] The boat which you build
... be equal ...
...
...
Roof her over like the depth,

[i.c30] so that the sun shall not see inside her.
Let her be roofed over fore and aft.
The gear should be very strong,

the pitch should be firm, and so give the boat strength.
I will shower down upon you later

[i.c35] a windfall of birds, a spate of fishes.'"
He opened the water clock and filled it,
he told it of the coming of the seven-day deluge.

Atrahasis and the Elders
Atrahasis received the command.
He assembled the Elders at his gate.

[i.c40] Atrahasis made ready to speak,
and said to the Elders:
"My god does not agree with your god,
Enki and Enlil are constantly angry with each other.
They have expelled me from the land.

[i.c45] Since I have always reverenced Enki,
he told me this.
I can not live in …
Nor can I set my feet on the earth of Enlil.
I will dwell with my god in the depths.

[i.c50] This he told me: …"

Construction of the Ark
[ii.10] The Elders …
The carpenter carried his axe,
the reedworker carried his stone,
the rich man carried the pitch,
the poor man brought the materials needed.

[Lacuna of about fifteen lines; the word Atraasis can be discerned.]

Boarding of the Ark
[ii.29] Bringing ...

[ii.30] whatever he had ...
Whatever he had ...
Pure animals he slaughtered, cattle ...
Fat animals he killed. Sheep ...
he choose and and brought on board.

[ii.35] The birds flying in the heavens,
the cattle and the ... of the cattle god,
the creatures of the steppe,
... he brought on board
...

[ii.40] he invited his people
... to a feast
... his family was brought on board.
While one was eating an another was drinking,

[ii.45] he went in and out; he could not sit, could not kneel,
for his heart was broken, he was retching gall.

Departure
The outlook of the weather changed.
Adadnote began to roar in the clouds.

[ii.50] The god they heard, his clamor.
He brought pitch to seal his door.
By the time he had bolted his door,
Adad was roaring in the clouds.
The winds were furious as he set forth,

[ii.55] He cut the mooring rope and released the boat.

[Lacuna]

The Great Flood
[iii.5] ... the storm
... were yoked
Anzu rent the sky with his talons,
He ... the land

[iii.10] and broke its clamor like a pot.
... the flood came forth.
Its power came upn the peoples like a battle,
one person did not see another,
they could not recognize each other in the catastrophe.

[iii.15] The deluge belowed like a bull,
The wind resounded like a screaming eagle.
The darkness was dense, the sun was gone,
... like flies.

[iii.20] the clamor of the deluge.

[Lacuna. The gods find themselves hungry because there are no farmers left and sacrifices are no longer brought. When they discover that Atrahasis has survived, they make a plan to make sure that the noise will remain within limits: they invent childbirth, infant mortality, and celibacy.]

Mankind Punished
[iii.45] Enki made ready to speak,
and said to Nintu the birth goddess:
"You, birth goddess, creatress of destinies,
establish death for all peoples!

> [iii.d1] "Now then, let there be a third woman among the people,
> among the people are the woman who has borne
> and the woman who has not borne.
> Let there be also among the people the pasittu (she-demon):
>
> [iii.d5] Let her snatch the baby from the lap who bore it.
> And etablish high priestesses and priestesses,
> let them be taboo,note and so cut down childbirth."

Each of these texts holds immense historical, cultural, and spiritual significance, providing religious guidance and insights into the moral and philosophical aspects of life as understood by their respective cultures. They remain subjects of study and reverence and continue to influence modern thought and spirituality today.

In the Mahabharata and Bhagavad Gita, the portrayal of divine intervention, wisdom, and power in human affairs might be interpreted as the actions of Anunnaki-like figures influencing and guiding humanity. Similarly, the Vedas's complex hierarchy of gods and their interactions with humans can be viewed through the lens of this hypothesis, offering a new perspective on these ancient deities.

The Egyptian Book of the Dead, with its detailed depiction of gods and the afterlife, presents another avenue for comparison. The roles and attributes of these deities can be analyzed in parallel with the Anunnaki's reputed characteristics, drawing intriguing connections between these two ancient cultures.

The Tibetan Book of the Dead, with its focus on the journey after death and the role of spiritual guides, provides yet another perspective. Thistext's deities and spiritual entities could be seen as analogs to the Anunnaki, guiding and influencing souls in the afterlife.

The Sumerian Tablets, which explicitly mention the Anunnaki, are key to this hypothesis. These tablets provide the most direct link, depicting the Anunnaki as powerful beings with significant influence over human destiny.

Anunnaki in Sumerian Mythology: The Anunnaki are primarily associated with Sumerian mythology. They were gods, descended from the sky, who were believed to have created and ruled over mankind. The idea that these gods were from another world or had superior knowledge and power is central to their depiction.

Similarities Across Cultures: I would like to point out similarities in the depiction of gods across various ancient cultures. For instance, gods in different mythologies often share characteristics like immense power, longevity, and a role in creating or guiding humanity.

Advanced Knowledge and Technology: Ancient texts often describe gods as possessing advanced knowledge and technology, which some interpret as evidence of extraterrestrial origin. This idea is bolstered by descriptions of flying machines, advanced weaponry, and otherworldly abilities. If you take the position that our ancient ancestors lacked the technical terminology to adequately describe what they saw or encountered, then you can begin discerning what truly happened. I believe our ancestors were engaged by several races of advanced beings that created a breakaway civilization on Earth.

Thoth is a prominent figure in ancient Egyptian mythology, known as the god of wisdom, writing, hieroglyphs, science, magic, art, judgment, and the dead. He is often depicted as a man with the head of an ibis or a baboon, animals sacred to him. His significance in Egyptian culture is profound, being credited with the invention of writing and serving as the scribe of the gods.

The Emerald Tablets of Thoth are a more esoteric subject and not a part of mainstream Egyptian mythology. They are said to be a set of emerald green tablets containing Thoth's wisdom. The texts, supposedly written by Thoth himself, are claimed to offer profound mystical insight. They are often associated with Hermeticism and alchemy and are considered a cornerstone in the Hermetic tradition.

Key Points about Thoth:

1. God of Wisdom and Knowledge: Thoth is revered as the god of wisdom, knowledge, and learning. He is often seen as the heart and tongue of Ra, the sun god, and the means by which Ra's will is translated.

2. The Scribe of the Gods: Thoth is the official scribe of the divine, keeping the records of all the gods and acting as an arbitrator in their disputes.

3. Association with the Afterlife: He plays a significant role in the afterlife, seen in the "Weighing of the Heart" ceremony, where he records the results of the judgments over the souls of the dead.

4. Depiction: Thoth is usually depicted as a man with the head of an ibis, holding a writing palette and reed pen, or as a baboon. These symbols represent wisdom, writing, and the measurement of time.

Emerald Tablets of Thoth:

1. Mystical Texts: The Emerald Tablets are described as containing secrets and esoteric knowledge. The texts are reputed to be immensely old and of great importance for hermetic and alchemical traditions.
2. Content: The tablets contain precepts and principles of alchemical transformation and deep philosophical insights and quantum physics. They discuss the nature of the universe, secrets of spiritual transformation, and paths to higher consciousness.
3. Cultural Impact: The Emerald Tablets have had a significant impact on Western esoteric thought, influencing various mystic and occult traditions for tens of thousands of years.

In my book *Compendium Of The Emerald Tablets* by Billy Carson, I break down the verses below in an attempt to help the reader discern the written evidence of advanced technology and supreme knowledge wielded by Thoth the Atlantean over 36,000 years ago. Read the following verses, and you will begin to understand that Thoth took a crew onto a ship that flies and then rebuilt a civilization in Khem (Egypt).

Excerpt from the Emerald Tablets of Thoth:

> Gathered I then my people and
> entered the great ship of the Master.

Upward we rose into the morning.
Dark beneath us lay the Temple.
Suddenly over it rose the waters.
Vanished from Earth,
until the time appointed,
was the great Temple.

Fast we fled toward the sun of the morning,
until beneath us lay the land of the children of KHEM.
Raging, they came with cudgels and spears,
lifted in anger seeking to slay and utterly destroy the Sons of Atlantis.

Then raised I my staff and directed a ray of vibration,
striking them still in their tracks as fragments of stone of the mountain.
Then spoke I to them in words calm and peaceful,
telling them of the might of Atlantis,
saying we were children of the Sun and its messengers.
Cowed I them by my display of magic-science,
until at my feet they groveled, when I released them.

Long dwelt we in the land of KHEM,
long and yet long again.
Until obeying the commands of the Master,
who while sleeping yet lives eternally,
I sent from me the Sons of Atlantis,
sent them in many directions,
that from the womb of time wisdom
might rise again in her children.
Long time dwelt I in the land of KHEM,
doing great works by the wisdom within me.
Upward grew into the light of knowledge
the children of KHEM,
watered by the rains of my wisdom.

The Mahabharata and Bhagavad Gita: In Hindu texts, gods like Krishna display remarkable powers and knowledge. The descriptions of the Vimana, flying chariots, and advanced weaponry in the Mahabharata are sometimes cited as evidence of advanced, possibly extraterrestrial technology.

Egyptian and Tibetan Texts: Similarly, in the Egyptian Book of the Dead and the Tibetan Book of the Dead, there are references to deities with significant powers and knowledge about life, death, and the afterlife, which some interpret as signs of a higher, possibly extraterrestrial intelligence.

Cultural Interpretation and Mythological Symbolism: Critics of this hypothesis argue that these similarities are not evidence of a common extraterrestrial origin but rather reflect a shared human tendency to mythologize the unknown. They suggest that ancient people used gods and mythology to explain natural phenomena, moral ideals, and existential questions. I personally believe that our ancestors were much more intelligent than is assumed. I believe that "MODERN" man (EGO) has used wishful thinking to disregard the accounts of our ancestors and the clear evidence of a race of advanced beings engaging mankind in the ancient past.

Archaeological and Historical Evidence: There is significant archaeological or historical evidence supporting the idea that the gods of these ancient texts were Anunnaki or extraterrestrial beings.

Here is a list of ancient temples and pyramids around the world that use megalithic building techniques that we cannot duplicate today using our "ADVANCED" technology.

Supposedly, our ancestors did this using a combination of mud, elephants, copper chisels, and chicken bones.

Megalithic Temples

1. **Göbekli Tepe**, Turkey: Göbekli Tepe is a fascinating archaeological site in Turkey that dates back to around 12,000 BCE. Considered one of the world's oldest temples, it was constructed using megalithic building techniques. The temple is decorated with intricate carvings of animals and humans and is thought to have been used for religious ceremonies.

2. **Ħaġar Qim and Mnajdra:** Malta Ħaġar Qim and Mnajdra are two megalithic temples located on the Maltese island of Malta. They were built between 3600 BCE and 2500 BCE, and they are considered to be some of the oldest freestanding structures in the world. The temples were constructed using massive stone blocks, some of which weighed over 20 tons.

3. **Stonehenge**, England: Stonehenge is a prehistoric monument located in Wiltshire, England. It is one of the most iconic megalithic structures in the world, and it has been a source of fascination for centuries. Stonehenge was constructed using massive stones arranged in a circular formation. The stones were transported to the site from over 20 miles away, and it is thought that the monument was built between 3000 BCE and 1500 BCE.

4. **The Baalbek stones** in Baalbek, Lebanon: The Baalbek stones are a collection of massive megalithic blocks that form part of the Temple of Jupiter Baal in Baalbek, Lebanon. They are some of the largest and heaviest stones ever used in construction, and they have been a source of fascination and speculation for centuries. The largest formation of the Baalbek stones is known as the Trilithon. The three massive stones that make up this structure each weigh around 800 tons and measure 19 meters (62 feet) long, 4.2 meters (14 feet) high, and 3.6 meters (12 feet) thick. The Trilithon is part of the podium of the Temple of Jupiter Baal. The other Baalbek stones are also impressive in their size and weight. Some of the stones weigh over 1,000 tons, and they are all cut and shaped with great precision. The stones are fitted together so tightly that there is no visible gap between them, and they have been able to withstand centuries of earthquakes and other natural disasters.

Megalithic Pyramids

1. **The Great Pyramids of Giza**, Egypt: The Great Pyramids of Giza are one of the most famous and impressive examples of megalithic construction. They were built over 4,000 years ago as tombs for the pharaohs Khufu, Khafre, and Menkaure. The pyramids were constructed using millions of stone blocks, some of which weigh over 2 tons.

2. **The Pyramid of Cholula**, Mexico: The Pyramid of Cholula is the largest pyramid in the world by volume. It is located in the Mexican state of Puebla, and it was built by the Toltec civilization. The pyramid was constructed using millions of adobe bricks, and it is thought to have been built between the 2nd and 7th centuries CE.

3. **The Bosnian Pyramid** in Bosnia & Herzegovina: This complex includes a group of five pyramids in central Bosnia and Herzegovina that are considered to be artificially shaped pyramids. The largest of these pyramids, Visočica Hill, is the centerpiece of the Bosnian Pyramid complex. It is claimed to be 220 meters (722 ft) tall, making it the tallest pyramid in the world.

These are just a few examples of the many ancient temples and pyramids around the world that use megalithic building techniques. These structures are a testament to the ingenuity and skill of ancient civilizations, and they continue to fascinate and amaze us today.

The Vedas are a collection of ancient Indian spiritual texts that form the foundation of Hinduism. They are among the oldest sacred texts in the world, written in Sanskrit and composed over a broad period, beginning as early as 1500 BCE. The Vedas are not just religious scriptures but also encompass a wide array of knowledge, including philosophy, science, and the arts.

Structure and Content of the Vedas:

1. **Rigveda**: The oldest of the Vedas, the Rigveda consists of 1,028 hymns dedicated to various deities. It's primarily a collection of hymns praising the Vedic gods, providing insights into the religious life of the early Vedic people.
2. **Samaveda**: Essentially a liturgical collection, the Samaveda consists mainly of hymns from the Rigveda set to musical chants. These hymns were sung during religious ceremonies and rituals.
3. **Yajurveda**: This Veda is more practical in its approach and contains rituals and ceremonies to be performed during sacrifices. It is a compilation of ritual offering formulas that were said by a priest.
4. **Atharvaveda**: The Atharvaveda is different from the other three Vedas and is more diverse in content, including hymns, chants, spells, and prayers. It addresses everyday life aspects, such as health, longevity, and material prosperity.

Each Veda is further subdivided into four parts: the Samhitas (mantras and hymns), the Brahmanas (ritualistic texts), the Aranyakas (texts on rituals, ceremonies, sacrifices, and symbolic sacrifices), and the Upanishads (philosophical texts discussing meditation, philosophy, and spiritual knowledge).

Indian Vedas: Wikipedia

Depiction of Vedic Gods and Parallels with Anunnaki:

The Vedic gods represent various natural and cosmic phenomena. For example, Indra is the god of rain and thunderstorms, Agni is the fire god, and Vayu is the wind god. Each god has specific characteristics and attributes, and they are revered through hymns and sacrifices.

In examining parallels with the Anunnaki of ancient Mesopotamian culture, several aspects can be considered:

1. Divine Hierarchy and Powers: Like the Anunnaki, the Vedic gods form a hierarchy and possess immense powers. They are involved in the creation, maintenance, and regulation of the cosmos, similar to the Anunnaki's role in Mesopotamian texts.

2. Interaction with Humanity: Both the Vedic gods and the Anunnaki are depicted as interacting with humans, influencing their lives, and guiding them, often imparting knowledge and laws.
3. Symbolism and Mythology: Both sets of deities are shrouded in mythology and symbolic representation. The stories and hymns often have deeper philosophical or spiritual meanings.
4. Technological Interpretation: In modern interpretations, some speculate about advanced technologies in ancient times, drawing parallels between descriptions of divine weapons and chariots in Vedic texts and the advanced technology supposedly possessed by the Anunnaki.

The Egyptian Book of the Dead is an ancient Egyptian funerary text used from the beginning of the New Kingdom (around 1550 BCE) to around 50 BCE. The original Egyptian name for the text, "rw nw prt m hrw," translates to "Book of Coming Forth by Day" or "Book of Emerging Forth into the Light." It's a collection of spells, prayers, and incantations designed to assist the deceased in their journey through the Duat (the underworld) and into the afterlife.

Key Aspects of the Egyptian Book of the Dead:

1. Collection of Spells and Incantations: The text is a compilation of various spells that were believed to protect the dead and guide them through the afterlife's challenges, ensuring a safe passage.

2. Journey Through the Afterlife: It describes the journey of the soul through the underworld, encountering various deities, demons, and challenges along the way.
3. The Weighing of the Heart Ceremony: One of the most significant aspects detailed in the Book of the Dead is the "Weighing of the Heart" ceremony, where the dead person's heart is weighed against the feather of Ma'at (truth and justice) to determine their worthiness for the afterlife.
4. Magical and Symbolic Elements: The text is filled with magical and symbolic elements intended to provide knowledge, protection, and power to the deceased in the afterlife.
5. Personalized for the Deceased: While there were standard versions, many copies of the Book of the Dead were customized for the individual deceased, including their name and titles.

Nature and Roles of Egyptian Deities and Comparison with Anunnaki:

Egyptian deities often represented natural elements or aspects of life and were deeply integrated into the daily life and afterlife beliefs of ancient Egyptians.

1. Roles and Characteristics: Egyptian gods, like Osiris, Anubis, Ra, and Isis, played specific roles in the cosmology of ancient Egypt, governing aspects of life, death, the underworld, and the cosmos.
2. Interaction with Humans: Similar to the Anunnaki, Egyptian deities interacted with humans, guiding and

influencing their lives and afterlives. Gods like Anubis and Osiris were directly involved in the afterlife journey of the deceased.

3. Anunnaki Comparison: The Anunnaki were considered higher beings with significant power and knowledge in ancient Mesopotamian texts. While both Egyptian deities and the Anunnaki were seen as powerful and influential, the nature of their influence differed. The Anunnaki were more involved in the creation and ruling of humanity, whereas Egyptian gods were more focused on the natural order, life, and the afterlife.

4. Symbolism and Mythology: Both cultures used rich symbolism and mythology to explain natural phenomena, the cosmos, and human existence. However, the nature of these mythologies was shaped by their distinct cultural and environmental contexts.

Zep Tepi, meaning "First Time" or "First Occasion," was a term used by the ancient Egyptians to refer to a golden age that existed before their own civilization. The ancient Egyptians said that the Netru (Sky-Gods) came down from the heavens and turned mud into a kingdom. It was a time of peace, prosperity, and harmony, when the gods ruled directly over the earth. The Egyptians believed that Zep Tepi was a time of great knowledge and wisdom, and they often looked back on it with nostalgia.

The Neteru depicted on the exterior walls of Edfu Temple in Egypt: Wikipedia

Here are some of the characteristics of Zep Tepi that the Ancient Egyptians believed in:

The gods ruled directly over the earth and interacted with humans on a regular basis.

There was no war or conflict.

People were healthy and long-lived.

There was an abundance of food and resources.

People were wise and knowledgeable.

The Egyptians believed that Zep Tepi ended when the gods withdrew from the earth and left humans to rule themselves. This was seen as a time of decline and degeneration. However, the Egyptians still held onto the hope that Zep Tepi would one day return.

In summary, while there are some broad similarities in the roles and attributes of Egyptian deities and the Anunnaki, they are distinct in their cultural contexts and specific mythologies. The Egyptian Book of the Dead, in particular, focuses more on the afterlife and moral judgment rather than the creation and direct governance of humanity, which is more prominent in the myths surrounding the Anunnaki.

The Sumerian Tablets are a collection of clay tablets inscribed with cuneiform script, one of the earliest known forms of writing, developed by the ancient Sumerians of Mesopotamia. These tablets, dating back to the late 4th millennium BCE, offer invaluable insights into the daily life, culture, mythology, and history of one of the world's earliest civilizations.

Mythological and Historical Narratives in Sumerian Tablets:

1. Mythology: Sumerian mythology is richly documented in these tablets. They contain creation myths, stories of gods and goddesses, and tales of heroic deeds. Notable among these are the Epic of Gilgamesh, the Enuma Elish (the Babylonian creation myth), and various myths involving gods like Enlil, Enki, and Inanna.

2. Historical Records: The tablets are NOT mythological; they serve as historical records. They include king lists, administrative records, legal codes, and economic transactions. These documents provide a detailed understanding of the social, political, and economic aspects of Sumerian society.

3. Literature and Education: Many tablets were used for educational purposes, containing lexical lists, mathematical calculations, and practice exercises for scribes. This reflects a highly sophisticated and literate culture that appeared out of nowhere.

Depiction of the Anunnaki in Sumerian Tablets:

The Anunnaki hold a prominent place in Sumerian mythology, as depicted in these ancient texts.

1. Nature of the Anunnaki: The Anunnaki are described as a group of deities associated with various aspects of the natural world and the cosmos. They were believed to be powerful beings who influenced the fate of humanity and the functioning of the universe.
2. Influence on Human Affairs: In Sumerian belief, the Anunnaki were deeply involved in human affairs. They were seen as the creators of mankind, a species they fashioned to serve the gods. Many of the myths involve the Anunnaki interacting with humans, sometimes helping them and at other times sending calamities.
3. Roles and Hierarchies: The Anunnaki had a hierarchical structure with gods like Anu, Enlil, and Enki at the top. These deities had specific roles, such as Enlil being the god of air and the king of the gods, while Enki was the god of water and wisdom.
4. Epic of Gilgamesh: One of the most famous Sumerian texts, the Epic of Gilgamesh, though not directly mentioning the Anunnaki, portrays a world where gods and humans interact closely, reflecting the broader

Mesopotamian belief system in which the Anunnaki played a significant role.

5. Interpretations and Legacy: The depiction of the Anunnaki has been subject to various interpretations over time. In some modern contexts, they have been linked to theories of ancient astronauts. Once you begin to analyze the ancient texts, tablets, cylinder scrolls, and scriptures recorded by our ancestors with an open mind, you can begin to discern the many accounts and physical evidence left for us to uncover.

In conclusion, the Sumerian Tablets provide a fascinating window into ancient Mesopotamian life and beliefs. The Anunnaki, as depicted in these texts, are central to understanding the Sumerian perception of the cosmos and their belief in the intimate involvement of deities in the natural world and human destiny. Their portrayal in these ancient narratives highlights the rich and complex mythology of one of the earliest known civilizations in human history.

Synthesizing the wisdom from these texts, the chapter explores the possibility that the gods described could be manifestations or interpretations of the Anunnaki. Themes of divine wisdom, power, control, and involvement in human warfare are discussed, drawing parallels and highlighting differences.

While acknowledging the speculative nature of this theory, it's thrilling to consider the diverse interpretations we've explored in the available historical, archaeological, and textual evidence. This exploration emphasizes the importance of interdisciplinary study, not just as an academic exercise but as a vital tool for deepening our understanding of ancient civilizations and their complex belief systems.

The insights from this comparative study help to guide us in our understanding of ancient religious and mythological narratives. By keeping an open mind when exploring the mysteries of the past, we invite a future ripe with discovery and understanding. These intriguing connections hold the keys to unlocking the vast, unexplored wisdom of our ancestors.

Stele of Ashurnasirpal II - Nimrud [Kalhu] : Billy Carson at the British Museum

Chapter 4 – Sunken Cities and Earth Catastrophes

By Matthew LaCroix

Ancient cultures around the world speak of a time when sophisticated -global civilizations once existed that were destroyed by a series of devastating Earth catastrophes. Their influences gave rise to the Predynastic civilizations of Egypt, the pre-Inca of South America, the Maya of Mexico, and many others across the planet. Despite the mainstream popularity of the Atlantean story, there is also evidence to show that other sophisticated civilizations existed during the same time period - such as Lemuria in the Pacific Ocean, or the Athenian culture that pre-dated the classical Greeks.

In my previous chapters, I went into detail explaining the destruction of the lost civilizations on Earth in deep antiquity. This chapter aims to go deeper into the cyclical nature of those catastrophes and how they caused the demise of these ancient civilizations around the world – many of which are now underwater today. Despite the perception that these stories are merely a myth in most of society, I will be providing compelling data to show they were in fact very real, and part of a lost chapter in human history - one that has been carried down by temple priests, elders, and mystics for thousands of years.

The first concept to incorporate when understanding this lost time period in human history is that ocean levels, climatic changes, and ice ages have played a major role in the rise and fall of ancient civilizations for thousands of years. Instead of the notion that the climate of Earth is constant and only affected by human influences, we should instead understand that cyclical changes are the only constant that exists. This is clearly apparent when one studies data taken from ice core samples from Greenland and Antarctica - which provides a frozen snapshot into what the Earth's climate was like over the last 20,000+ years. What the data shows is that the planet has undergone massive cycles of intense warming and cooling at certain time intervals, with relatively stable climatic patterns in between. These cooling and warming cycles usually last several thousand years, bringing with them either ice ages or rapidly melting glaciers, leading to ocean current, sea level, and climate disruptions.

These more 'stable' climatic time periods coincide closely with the rise of civilizations, while the latter often leads to their demise. This cycle on Earth typically occurs every 13,000 years, and is the result of two primary factors:
- Massive solar/electromagnetic changes from the sun due to the influences of a binary companion star
- Galactic/planetary energies coinciding

I think it's important to mention that a third, but less understood aspect of this cycle is related to comet and meteor impacts. However, the relative frequency of when those events occur is still largely unknown. Astronomical discoveries in the outer Solar System point to disruptions to the Kuiper Belt and Taurid meteor shower as a likely source.

This means that the cyclical nature of the climatic changes on the Earth follow the same cyclical nature seen within the rise and fall of civilizations on Earth – their fates being one and the same. However, it's important to understand that the disappearance of these past civilizations is not simply from climatic disruptions, but something far more destructive. This is because in-between those cycles of rapid warming and cooling, there is often a great catastrophe that occurs, or multiple catastrophes over a 1,000+ year period.

Geologic and climatologic evidence points to these catastrophes primarily being the result of pole shifts/electromagnetic disruptions to the Earth. The reason for this is due to what's known as the geomagnetic balance of the Earth, where the planets land masses and tectonic plates are maintained through a balance of its north and south magnetic poles. If those poles significantly shift due to a large coronal mass ejection (CME) from the sun, the results can be disastrous. Imagine for a moment what would happen if one of these events were to occur today. Severe climatic disruptions would be followed by gradual destabilization of the planet's tectonic plates, leading to devastating volcanoes and earthquakes that would culminate into tsunamis thousands of feet high that would rapidly sweep across the Earth - destroying everything in their path. Not only that, but if the geomagnetic poles are disturbed enough, there is a chance that holes will open up in the ozone layer that could allow powerful solar radioactive particles to pass through, incinerating any life on the surface from temperatures exceeding a two thousand degrees. This severe scarring or vitrification is evidence on ancient statues and structures around the world - such as the Colossi of Memnon in Egypt, where visible burned or melted rock can be observed.

On top of that, we also have direct evidence to show that the deluge story discussed in cuneiform tablets - such as the *Atra-Hasis* or *Epic of Gilgamesh*, was a real event which wiped out the pre-diluvian cities of ancient Mesopotamia, and other cultures around the world. That flood evidence can be found at the Ziggurat of Eridu, also known as the Temple of E-abzu, where large amounts of sea-shells have been photographed strewn across the ruins of this ancient temple complex, as well as signs of vitrification. Considering that Eridu is mentioned in numerous cuneiform tablets as being the *first* city created by the Anunnaki here, it makes logical sense that it would have existed well before the disastrous events of the Young Dryas period - roughly 12,800 years ago.

The presence of hundreds of sea-shells on the top of the Ziggurat in Eridu, Iraq is indicative of how powerful this deluge event was, with tsunami-like flood waters coming down both from the Black Sea to the north, as well as from the Persian Gulf to the south. These flood waters likely converged somewhere in Mesopotamia, depositing the sea-shells on the mountain temple before finally receding. That's why the tablets state that each pre-diluvian city created in Sumer was destroyed in a great deluge, leading to kingship being re-lowered in the city of Kish. This deluge story is described well in the *Epic of Gilgamesh*, where on **Tablet 11** it states:

> "The sky turned into darkness.
> [then came] the [Deluge.]
> Like a battle [the cataclysm] pass over the people.
> One man could not discern another,
> nor could people be recognized amid the destruction.
> Even the gods took fright at the Deluge,
> they left and went up to the heaven of Anu,
> lying like dogs curled up in the open.
> The goddess cried out like a woman in childbirth,
> Belet-ili wailed, whose voice is so sweet:
> 'The olden times have turned to clay,
> because I spoke evil in the gods' assembly.
> How could I speak evil in the gods' assembly,
> and declare a war to destroy my people?
> It is I who give birth, these people are mine!
> And now, like fish, they fill the ocean!'
> The Anunnaki gods were weeping with her,
> For six days and [seven] nights,
> the gale, the Deluge, it flattened the land.
> All the gods shall come to the incense,
> But to the incense let Enlil not come,

> *Because he lacked counsel and brought on the Deluge and delivered my people into destruction."*

The account of the Deluge in the *Epic of Gilgamesh* mirrors very closely with what's described in the *Atra-Hasis*, giving credibility to the authenticity of the story. Notice how it states that Enlil was the one who decided to bring on the Deluge to destroy mankind, which correlates with how that being is described in numerous ancient texts. This shows the division that exists within these Anunna gods over what the future of humanity should be and how important we are.

These cyclical disasters are the very reason why so many ancient civilizations - such as the Predynastic Egyptians, built enormous pyramids on specific locations on the planet in order to try and balance these cyclical disruptions. However, despite their best efforts, those civilizations would inevitably suffer the same fate as their ancestors – becoming nearly forgotten and lost to history. That's why today we find that most megalithic structures around the world that existed before the Younger Dryas events are off by 23.5 degrees to true north, since this were built before the axis of the planet shifted 12-13,000 years ago.

One of the most significant concepts to incorporate when understanding these ancient civilizations is the role that the oceans have played. Just as the climate is constantly changing, so too are ocean levels. Imagine you were alive 13,000 years ago, living near the coast in one of the numerous ancient cities that are now underwater. You would have experienced sea levels that were 400 feet lower than they are today. This led many of these cities to become submerged underwater as ocean levels rose due to rapid melting of the ice caps across North America and Europe/Asia. The following is a list of the most significant sunken cities/civilizations that have been either discovered or discussed in ancient texts:

- Atlantis
- Lemuria
- Dwarka off the western coast of India
- The sunken city of Thônis- Heracleion - located 30 feet underwater off the coast of Egypt
- Pavlopetri, Greece
- Yonaguni Monument, Japan (?)
- Sunken city off Pinar del Rio Province in Cuba

Atlantis

In the famous writings known as the *Timaeus and Critias*, the philosopher Plato described a grand civilization known as Atlantis that once existed somewhere west of the Pillars of Heracles, which was eventually destroyed by devastating catastrophes. Many modern academics have disregarded the story Plato gave as being nothing more than a clever allegory and not based on real events in the past.

The first evidence for the existence of Atlantis originated from Egypt, after the Athenian lawmaker and poet Solon traveled to the region in 600 BC, and learned about the story from priests at the Temple of Sais in the Nile Delta region. The Egyptian priests went into great detail about the civilization of Atlantis and its downfall, telling Solon that those "sacred records" had been kept within the Temple of Sais for thousands of years.

Credibility for this account from the priests of the Temple of Sais comes from the Greek historian Diodorus Siculus, who claims that the temple existed before the deluge, and that it was originally built by the Athenians - specifically Athena. Diodorus states that the Temple of Sais survived a great deluge and the records of Atlantis were preserved there for thousands of years. The Temple priests of Sais go on to explain to Solon that:

> *"There have been, and there will be again, many destructions of mankind arising out of many causes; the greatest have been brought about by fire and water. You remember a single deluge only, but there were many previous ones."*

Thankfully, the knowledge Solon was told by the ancient Egyptians did not die with him, but lived on through Diodorus and the works of Plato in the *Timaeus and Critias* - which still represent the most significant source of Atlantean knowledge we still have today. The *Timaeus* begins by explaining the parameters needed for a perfect society, in which ancient Athens is used as a comparison to the civilization of Atlantis. Solon goes on to explain that Atlantis was a vast and powerful maritime empire that became morally corrupt and had subjected its people to slavery. In the *Timaeus* Plato discusses Atlantis stating:

"For the ocean there was at that time navigable; for in front of the mouth which you Greeks call, as you say, 'pillars of

Heracles' there lay an island which was larger than Libya and Asia together; and it was possible for travelers of that time to cross from it to other islands, and from the island to the whole of the continent over against them which encompasses that veritable ocean."

> "For all that we have here, lying within the mouth of which we speak, is evidently a haven having a narrow entrance; but yonder is a real ocean, and the land surrounding it my most rightly be called, in the fullest and truest sense, a continent."

> "Now on this island of **Atlantis** there existed a confederation of kings of great and marvelous power, which held sway over all the island, and over many other islands and parts of the continent."

The Temple priests of Sais went into great detail about what Atlantis looked like when discussing it with Solon, describing it as an island with mountains in the north and a vast plain to the south - 345 miles in width. The central city was located south of the northern large mountain range which was connected to the ocean to the south-west, through a series of interconnected moats. They describe it as 3 large moats, with 2 circular land masses and an island in the center, where the Temple of Poseidon was located.

The Greek historian Diodorus Siculus described details about Atlantis and where it was located stating:

> "Atlantis is an island of considerable size, a number of days' voyage to the west... the dwelling-place of a race of gods [Giants], not men. In ancient times this island remained undiscovered, because of its distance from the other inhabitants of the world..."

Diodorus continues by explaining that Atlantis is a mountainous land, with a vast and beautiful plain in the southern part. This is important because it's precisely how Plato and Solon described it. One of the most interesting pieces of information that connects to these legends of giant kings and powerful bloodlines comes from the *Timaeus*, when Plato describes the kings of Atlantis saying:

> "a confederation of kings of great and marvelous power, which held sway over all the island, and over many other islands and parts of the continent."

This information correlates with how this 'confederation of kings' is described by both Plato in the *Critias*, as well as the Greek historian Diodorus, which state that these royal bloodline kings who ruled Atlantis we're all sons of Atlas, a divine ruler who is described as being the son of Poseidon. This is supported by the ancient Greek name of *Atlantis nesos*, which means "island of Atlas." Plato explains that Atlas was considered a demi-god since his mother was a mortal woman named Cleito, and father Poseidon was an immortal god.

In his book *Interpretation of Mycenaean Greek texts*, Leonard Palmer suggests a connection between Poseidon and the Sumerian god Enki, stating that the name Poseidon is a direct translation of "calque" meaning: 'lord of the earth", which is what EN-KI means in Sumerian. Furthermore, in the *Critias* Plato describes how Atlantis went to war with its competing maritime empire; the Athenians, who controlled the northern Mediterranean Sea, while Atlantis controlled the Atlantic, as well as parts of Africa, including Egypt. Both of these empires were competing for power and the patron god of the Athenians was Zeus -who is considered the Sumerian equivalent of Enlil. Cuneiform tablets clearly state that both of these gods were constantly in competition with one another. Is this ancient war between Atlantis and Athens a continuation of a competition between these ancient Mesopotamian gods – referred to as the war of the Titans versus the Olympians?

The other interesting correlation regarding Atlantean kings and connections with ancient Mesopotamia, comes from the comparing the progenitors of the pre-diluvian kings mentioned in the *Sumerian King List* and *Uruk List of Kings and Sages* tablets. These royal bloodlines can be traced all the way back to the Anunnaki, which are the same source of the Atlantean kings mentioned by the temple priests of Sais and Diodorus. That's why when you read about extreme longevity or special powers possessed by specific kings or sages, it always connects back to the Anunnaki, since they are the direct source of these gifts in humanity. This is the reason why so many elite-secret societies throughout history have been so focused on bloodlines.

In the *Critias*, Plato explains that the Athenians led a campaign against Atlantis, liberating the occupied lands it had conquered from the empire. During this war, destructive earth changes were occurring and it was described that parts of the main island of Atlantis were breaking apart and disappearing into the ocean. In the *Emerald Tablets*, Thoth mentions how the central island of Undall was one of the last remaining parts of the continent, before the sages and mystics fled to create new civilizations in other parts of the world - primarily Egypt. The

Critas goes into detail about these catastrophic events that led to the destruction of Atlantis stating:

> "But afterwards there occurred violent earthquakes and floods; and in a single day and night of misfortune all your warlike men in a body sank into the earth, and the island of Atlantis in like manner disappeared in the depths of the sea. For which reason the sea in those parts is impassable and impenetrable, because there is a shoal of mud in the way; and this was caused by the subsidence of the island."

In 1882, American Congressman and writer Ignatius L. Donnelly published the book: *Atlantis: The Antediluvian World*, in which he presented evidence to show that a sophisticated civilization known as Atlantis had once existed that was destroyed from the same event in the Bible known as the Great Flood. He based this theory on both Solon's descriptions of Atlantis and the date of its destruction - as well as studying the Maya civilization, who he believed had a common origin back to Atlantis and Egypt. Ignatius Donnelly goes on to state that he believed that the gods and goddesses of the Phoenicians, Greeks, Hindu people, and Scandinavians were the kings, queens, and heroes of Atlantis, and that some of those languages - especially the Phoenician alphabet, was originally derived from the Atlantis alphabet.

There has been great speculation regarding the location of where Atlantis used to exist. Plato and Solon described it as being found just west of the Pillars of Hercules stating:

> "There was an island situated in front of the straits which you call the Pillars of Heracles; the island was larger than Libya and Asia put together."

Researchers agree that the Pillars of Heracles is referring to what we know today as the Straits of Gibraltar. Based on this locational information, as well as how Atlantis is described as being destroyed by a violent series of earthquakes, most researchers historically agree that it was likely found somewhere along the Mid Atlantic Ridge, perhaps near the Azores Islands. This area has been shown to be geologically unstable, producing numerous volcanic and seismic events throughout history, due to being located at the confluence of three tectonic plates.

This general consensus among many historians and researchers on the location of Atlantis led to numerous maps being created, dating all the way back to 1669 when Athanasius Kircher produced the *Mundus Subterraneus map*, which placed Atlantis in the middle of the Atlantic Ocean. Since then, other maps have confirmed that location as well; such as the *Atlantis: The Antediluvian World* map created by Ignatius Donnelly in 1882, the William Scott-Elliott's *The Story of Atlantis* map created in 1910, or Damanhur's *Atlantis Map* created from memory recollection. This provides us with a probable location for where it likely was, somewhere along the mid-Atlantic Ridge, near the Azores Islands.

Edgar Cayce has famously discussed his clairvoyant abilities in remembering past lives relating to Atlantis, claiming that the human race is based on polygenism, where five different root races (white, black, red, brown, and yellow) were created around the world at different times. He states that Atlantis was the original home of the red race, who developed rapidly to become an advanced civilization that ruled over a large territory. He also believes that extraterrestrial beings were involved in the creation of Atlantis, and states that some of these 'beings' he calls "soul-entities" intermingled with proto-humans on Earth to create giants that were as much as twelve feet tall.

Cayce goes on to explain that Atlantis was in possession of certain technologies - such as a giant crystal which harnessed the energy of the sun, that was used to provide power to Atlantis. One of the reasons that Atlantis was destroyed was from a misuse of this crystal. Cayce states that the sages who survived Atlantis would eventually create the civilizations of Egypt, and that there is a "Hall of Records" beneath the Great Sphinx that contains the historical texts of Atlantis.

Today, we find evidence that supports Cayce's claims in Egypt, where at least three separate entrances have been found in and around the Great Sphinx, which supposedly lead down into tunnels that connect to the Hall of Records. These tunnels have been kept off-limits to the public, and numerous photographs have been taken showing Zahi Hawass (the previous head of Egyptian Antiquities) and other officials climbing down some of the stairways inside these shafts. Today, no one actually knows where they lead, but many experts believe they connect to a massive network of subterranean tunnels that exists under the Great Pyramids of Giza and surrounding areas.

The *Emerald Tablets* of Thoth states that the early civilizations of Egypt were founded by a being known as Thoth the Atlantean, who created a grand civilization in Egypt known as Kemet or the Land of Khem, and that the tunnels under the Great Sphinx lead to what he refers to as the Halls of Amenti. Thoth states that one of the reasons that Atlantis was destroyed was because certain groups there were practicing black magick and misusing energy for weapons technology. Thoth - along with his trusty sages and mystics, fled the island before it was destroyed and built the great pyramids.

The stories of Atlantis have captivated the minds of historians for centuries. A nearly forgotten epoch of human history that was all but erased from our memories due to devastating earth catastrophes. A land full of mystery and magick, where great gods lived side by side with humans, and left behind one of the greatest stories ever told.

As I discussed in a previous chapter, Plato states that the Atlantean civilization was destroyed in a single day by devastating catastrophes 9,000 years before he existed. Based on historical data we have for when Plato lived, this would place Atlantis's destruction on a timeline around 12,000 years ago. These details provided by Plato and Solon describing when Atlantis was destroyed lines up precisely with the violent Earth changes/climate disruptions of the Younger Dryas period.

Some researchers have argued that Atlantis may have been a literal break-away civilization that achieved even a higher sophistication than our own. One of the best pieces of evidence that supports that theory can be found in the Temple of Seti in Abydos, Egypt, where there exists a pillar of stone that contains strange hieroglyphs that strikingly resemble a modern plane, helicopter, and submarine. Most mainstream academics argue that these hieroglyphs were re-carved, and aren't authentic. However, I believe that excuse is simply a way to discredit their significance, since they are what's known as "out of place artifacts" that do not fit in with the proposed timeline of civilizations taught in history books. Furthermore, even if it was true that they were re-carved by a later culture, how exactly would that culture have known about planes, helicopters, and submarines - hundreds if not thousands of years ago? The only logical conclusion is that the knowledge of these machines was handed down to them from a much more ancient and sophisticated civilization.

Those who objectively study the history of early Egypt know that there is compelling evidence to show that a much older and more sophisticated civilization existed in the region known as the Kemesians, whose name is derived from the original name for the region they called: The Land of Khem or Khemit. The Kemesians are credited as being the direct descendants of the Atlantean's, according to Greek historians and Egyptian priests. Ancient texts state that before Atlantis was destroyed, a group of enlightened priest and masons traveled to the Nile Delta of Egypt, to create a grand civilization there using sophisticated technology from Atlantis. That's why modern academics have no idea how structures like the Great Pyramid were even created, since they likely date to the same time period as these other lost civilizations.

Sunken City off Cuba

There are many researchers who believe that the search for Atlantis should include the Caribbean islands and Yucatan region of eastern Mexico. This theory is based on the idea that the Maya and Caribbean cultures had connections and influences back to the Atlantean Civilization. That's why when one of the most significant underwater discoveries ever made occurred off the western coast of Cuba in 2001, many became convinced it was the remnants of Atlantis.

With so many stories speaking of great deluges from ancient cultures and indigenous people around the world, the question is not if these sunken cities exist, but *where* they located. With only around 5% of the total ocean floor explored, we're just beginning to discover them today. That's why when marine engineers Pauline Zalitzki and Paul Weinzweig were hired by the Cuban government in 2001 to explore the ocean floor for old treasure ships and oil reserves, they would accidentally stumble across something that could potentially change all of history...

Located off the western tip of Cuba, in the Pinar del Río Province of Cuba lies a 2,000 foot deep - sandy plateau that extends for miles. The area was of great interest to the Cuban Government, who hired Zalitzki and Weinzweig to thoroughly explore the region using extensive sonar scans and video analysis. At more than 2,000 feet below the surface, the pressure is too strong for divers, which means that using sonar or remote operated vehicles is the only option. Utilizing an electronic tether, pulsing sound waves combed the seabed looking for any trace of sunken ships. As Zalitzki and Weinzweig watched the monitor, large artificially looking objects appeared, which closely resembled pyramids and geometrically precise structures.

Baffled by what they saw, the magnitude of the discovery grew to what appeared to be a large urban center stretching an astounding 12 miles across. The ruins appeared to be composed of large-megalithic stone blocks. Some of the structures within the complex were well over a thousand feet long and over a hundred feet tall. The stone blocks formed what appeared to be the outline of rooms, corridors, and pyramid-like shaped structures.

Sunken city off the coast of Cuba: Wikipedia
Coordinates: 21°46'21"N 84°50'12"W
21.772547°N 84.836736°W

Zelitsky and Weinzweig discussed their initial reactions to the sonar images in interviews where they said: *"We were shocked, and frankly we were a little frightened. The sea bottom in that area is an undulating sand plain. What we were seeing should not have been there. Our first thought was maybe we found some kind of secret military installation."*

Over the next 6 months Zelitsky and Weinzweig were silent about their discovery, worried what would happen if they spoke up about it. Zelitsky suddenly had an epiphany one day stating: *"Then one day, in our office, I looked up and saw pictures of ancient Mexican ruins on a calendar, and I made a mental connection."*

This realization that the ruins may be related to an ancient civilization led Zelitsky and Weinzweig to return to the site in July of 2001, this time with the help of geologist Manuel Iturralde. Manuel Iturralde - a senior researcher of Cuba's National History Museum, was considered highly qualified by many and brought onto the project to validate the significance of the discovery and better understand it.

This time, instead of only using sonar, the team also brought with them a Remotely Operated Vehicle to examine the area and film the findings. As the Remotely Operated Vehicle approached the site, giant 8-10-foot-tall blocks of what appeared to be hewn granite, came into view. Most were stacked on top of one another, with numerous blocks strewn around the site. In an area of the sea floor composed of mostly sand, these structures dramatically stood out due to their prominence. As the Remotely Operated Vehicle surveyed the ruins, cube and pyramid-like structures, and other complex buildings came into view.

Paul Weinzweig said in an interview that the underwater Cuban ruins are like: *"Some kind of megaliths you'd find on Stonehenge or Easter Island."*

Pauline Zalitzki said that the images appeared to reflect the ruins of a submerged city but was: *"reluctant to draw any conclusions without further evidence."* Weinzweig continued by saying: *"We've shown them to scientists in Cuba, the U.S., and elsewhere, and nobody has suggested they are natural."*

The geologist Manuel Iturralde commented about the Remotely Operated Vehicle footage stating: *"These are extremely peculiar structures, and they have captured our imagination, but if I had to explain this geologically, I would have a hard time."* What he means by that, is that according to his understanding of the geologic history of the region, if these structures were artificially made, they would have had to be created around 50,000 years ago - due to the depth they are found. Iturralde goes on to explain: *"50,000 years ago there wasn't the architectural capacity in any of the cultures we know of to build complex buildings."*

Of course, this perspective is based on the mainstream historical narrative, which confidently states that the furthest back human civilization goes is ~6,000 years old. This evidence - along with so many other discoveries around the world, is pushing that narrative back by thousands of years.

Iturralde did add, however, that there are local legends from the Maya and Yucatecos people, that tell of an island inhabited by their ancestors that disappeared beneath the ocean. Could this be that same island? An expert in underwater archaeology at Florida State University commented about the sunken Cuban ruins saying: *"It would be cool if they were right, but it would be real advanced for anything we would see in the New World for that time frame. The structures are out of time and out of place."*

News of the discovery quickly spread across the media where many drew parallels to connect back to the lost civilization of Atlantis. However, Zelinsky and Weinzweig felt that the ruins had more in common with the Maya of Mexico stating: *"What we have found is more likely remnants of a local culture,"* once located on a 100-mile *"*land bridge*"* that joined Mexico's Yucatan Peninsula with Cuba.*"*

This theory also correlates with the local legends of the Maya and Yucatecos cultures described by Iturralde. The data certain brings one to seriously ponder whether the civilizations of Atlantis and the Maya were both connected long ago in deep antiquity. However, the underlying question remains: "How could these ruins have reached a depth of over 2,000 feet below the surface of the ocean?"

According to geologist Randall Carson and researcher Brien Foerster, the Earth has seen continuous cycles of catastrophes on a scale unlike anything in modern history. From cosmic impacts to massive coronal mass ejections and pole shifts, each of these events dramatically impacted the surface of the planet. Evidence shows that large tectonic shifts, earthquakes, and volcanoes have the ability to significantly alter or destroy entire landmasses. Geologists postulate that a major tectonic event could have led to significant subduction of parts of the planet - including the plate that the sunken city off Cuba is located on today. The St. Petersburg Times agreed with this theory stating: *"This site, perhaps built by a culture that far predates the famous Maya of the Yucatan Peninsula, might have been the victim of a vast, mysterious cataclysm that somehow dropped it 2,000 feet beneath the surface of the sea."*

There is other evidence that supports those conclusions as well, such as in 2020, when archeologists diving in Mexico's Yucatan Peninsula discovered 12,000-year-old ochre mines that would pre-date the conventional time period of the classic Maya by thousands of years. They were able to determine that by finding evidence of hand tools, and ash - likely used for light, to access the ochre deposits located over 2,000 feet into the cave systems. What makes this site so important in the context of the sunken Cuban ruins, is that these ochre deposits are now deep under the ocean, and can only be reached using air tanks and diving equipment. This provides further evidence to show that the Maya civilization is much older than we're told, and that ocean levels were significantly lower when these deposits were being mined.

Further evidence that supports a lost civilization in this region was found in 1986, when three divers named Joseph Valentine, Jacques Mayol, and Robert Angove discovered what appeared to be an ancient underwater pathway near the Bahamas that became known as the "Bimini Road", due to its proximity to North Bimini Island. The Bimini Road is a set of unusual rock anomalies that feature "pavement-like" linear characteristics that run parallel to a set of stone walls that are composed of flat-rectangular, polygonal limestone blocks. At half a mile long and 18 feet below the ocean surface, the Bimini Road has captivated geologists, archeologists, and engineers since its discovery. Due to the degree of straightness and evenly spaced blocks, some have theorized that it acted as an ancient road for cultures in the region.

The experts are divided in their opinions on whether the Bimini Road is natural or artificial, since severe erosion of the blocks has worn off any potentially tool marks. However, I feel that after studying bathometric charts and extensively reviewing the evidence, that the Bimini Road is indeed man-made and likely functioned as a trading route or thoroughfare when ocean levels were much lower. The implications that would come along with these structures being man-made would challenge the entire doctrine of history, providing evidence to show that the people of the Bahamas region likely arrived far earlier than thought, and may have been connected all the way back to the Maya civilization of the Yucatan, and possibly Atlantis - long ago in the past.

Clearly, the history of civilizations in Mexico and the Caribbean is complex and ancient - existing well over 12,000 years ago, and containing similar symbolism to other cultures around the world, such as Mesopotamia and Egypt. That's the reason why so many researchers; such as Graham Hancock and Andrew Collins, looked to the America's for evidence of Atlantis, since so much evidence shows that they may have been connected. This excitement about a potential sunken city off Cuba - connected to Atlantis, led to great interest from National

Geographic Magazine and the Cuban National Museum. The senior editor at National Geographic - John Echave, traveled down to the region and said: *"They are interesting anomalies, but that's as much as anyone can say right now. But I'm no expert on sonar, and until we are able to actually go down there and see, it will be difficult to characterize them."*

Despite detailed sonar images taken and geologic analysis from experts around the world; who overwhelmingly agreed these were clearly man-made structures, no further investigations were **ever** done of the sunken city off Cuba, and the discovery was seemingly forgotten. Instead, these incredible underwater ruins left behind from an ancient civilization will remain thousands of feet below the surface, waiting for a time when they can finally be studied and fully understood by an aware and open-minded society.

In the end, it seems clear to me that many of the lost civilizations around the world that mysterious disappeared more than 12,000 years ago, where connected in some way to Atlantis. However, it would be irresponsible to conclude this chapter without at least briefly discussing another famous continent/civilization that has been woven into local legends, ancient stories, and preserved in sacred libraries known as *Lemuria/Mu*.

Lemuria/Mu

Lemuria - sometimes called Mu, is a legendary lost continent of the Pacific Ocean that was destroyed more than 12,000 years ago. However, unlike Atlantis, there are far fewer written records that managed to survive from this mysterious civilization. Instead, we rely on a combination of indigenous stories, ancient maps, and possible archeological ruins that remains scattered throughout the Pacific region.

Lemuria is described as a grand civilization that existed in the Pacific Ocean at the same time period as Atlantis in the Atlantic. Each civilization was highly sophisticated and technological in certain ways, but very different in terms of societal values and structure. Lemuria was based on the values of living harmoniously with the Earth and non-materialism, whereas Atlantis became war-like and turned into an empire. That's not to say Atlantis didn't contain brilliant sages or that it began that way, just that it eventually became corrupted.

Arguably the best written evidence that discusses details about Lemuria comes from an unlikely place - Tibet. Located beneath the massive Himalayan Mountains, the shamans and monks of Tibet have preserved the history of Lemuria in their ancient records for thousands of years. Strict rules meant that few outsiders were ever allowed in - in order to not pollute the story. However, that would all change with a man named James Churchward.

James Churchward - an American writer and engineer, dedicated much of his life to traveling the world. He spent a great deal of his time studying with the Rishis of India and the shamans and monks of Tibet, reading ancient texts and learning the esoteric secrets of the past. While studying in a sacred Indian/Tibetan monastery, he was told a fantastic story about a continent that became lost under the ocean called Lemuria or Mu. He was fascinated by what he was told and decided to dedicate his time to learning the secrets about this lost civilization. After years of research - spending time with the monks and shamans of India/Tibet, he wrote his first book called: *"The lost Continent of Mu..."* which provided the first glimpse into this nearly forgotten story.

He writes about how the story of Lemuria/Mu had been almost lost to even the shamans and monks due to how old it was. Then, in 1900, a Taoist monk made an astonishing discovery in a set of cliffside caves – in a place called Dunhuang, located in northern Tibet. What the monk found was worth more than gold or precious gems, for he had stumbled across an ancient library - containing the accumulated knowledge of thousands of years of Indian/Tibetan history. The contents of this ancient library had been preserved for more than 800 years - due to the dry, desert climate of the region.

Churchward explains that one day, an explorer and archaeologist named Sir Aurel Stein, passed through the area in 1907 and happened to meet the monk who had discovered the library. He persuaded the monk to allow him to see the secret library - which remained hidden within its cliffside cave, by explaining that he was an expert in reading ancient texts and could verify the significance of the library's contents. The monk decided to trust him, leading him up the treacherous path to reach the library.

What Stein found was a collection of ancient Buddhist texts, composed of numerous languages such as: Chinese, Tibetan, and Sanskrit. As Stein carefully peeled back the fragile pages and studied the texts, his excitement grew as he noticed that one of the manuscripts had what appeared to be fragments of an ancient map concealed inside. To his amazement, the map contained depictions of two lost continents/civilizations that once existed in the Atlantic and Pacific Oceans - known as Atlantis and Lemuria. That map, shown below, would eventually be included in his 1931 book: *Lemuria—Lost Continent in the Pacific.*

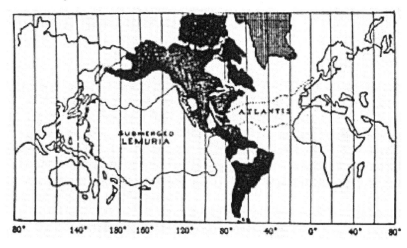

After spending a great deal of time carefully studying this map, I have come to the conclusion that it may be the **most** important ancient map ever discovered. It contains important depictions relating to ocean levels 12,000 years ago, inland flooding in North and South America, as well as the location of where lost civilizations once existed around the world. Notice the word "submerged" is used regarding Lemuria. This implies that the entire landmass sank and disappeared into the sea. This could only have occurred from a massive tectonic shift - on a scale beyond our current comprehension, in conjunction with a rapid melting of the ice caps. These events likely contributed to a catastrophic subduction of the Lemurian continent in the Pacific Ocean, and later the Atlantean landmasses.

These violent tectonic events contributed to the subduction of other areas of the planet as well; such as the sunken city off Cuba and eventually Atlantis. Not only that, but the map also depicts the aftermath of the devastating flooding that occurred in parts of North and South America - such as the Amazon and Mississippi River basins from worldwide tsunamis that swept the globe. These flood waters would have been slow to recede in these low-lying areas, which is why they are still shown underwater.

That's one of the reasons why I put so much emphasis on the importance of this map, since it precisely lines up with how ancient records, ice-core samples, and geologic evidence depicts what the world looked like during the Younger Dryas events of 12-13,000 years ago. That correlating evidence presents an opportunity for humanity to piece together a timeline of our past - in order to finally understand everything that came before this current epoch, as well as recognizing the ancient struggles we've been through.

After the destruction of the continent, the remnants of Lemuria were fractured into the island mountain tops of Easter Island, Polynesia, Micronesia, Melanesia, New Zealand, Indonesia, and Hawaii. That meant that the only archeological evidence that could have survived (above the ocean) would have been whatever was built in these specific locations. That's why many of the indigenous cultures of the region have legends that state that those survivors migrated to high elevation locations in the region to preserve that ancient knowledge from being lost.

After extensively studying ancient ruins and statues around the world, I have come to the conclusion that the most likely archeological evidence that still remains from the Lemurian civilization is found in four places: Easter Island, Indonesia, Peru and Bolivia. However, for the purposes of this chapter, I will be primarily focusing on Easter Island and Indonesia, but still discussing Peru and Bolivia in conjunction with those locations.

Easter Island

The mysterious ruins found on Easter Island have drawn archeologists and visitors to its remote shores for centuries. From the hundreds of mysterious Moai statues found throughout the island, to precise - megalithic walls such as Ahu Vinapu, the history of Easter Island is far more complex than history books tell us. According to indigenous legends, Easter Island was once part of the lost continent known as Lemuria/Mu; also called Hiva by some, before it succumbed to devastating tectonic catastrophes that caused to it sink beneath the Pacific Ocean. The island landmass of Easter Island was likely far enough away and high enough in elevation to avoid total destruction.

Easter Island is most famous for the over 800 Moai statues that dot its volcanic landscape. Just like many other ancient locations around the world, evidence shows that the Rapa Nui civilization were not the original builders of the monolithic and megalithic structures on the island, and probably found them when they colonized the region. This means that many of the largest Moai statues (some more than 40 feet tall) are likely much older than credited – dating to before the Younger Dryas catastrophes. Evidence to support this comes from the numerous archeological digs that have been conducted on the island over the last 20+ years, which have shown that many of these Moai statues are buried by upwards of 30 feet of sediment. This large amount of sediment was likely deposited over the course of thousands of years, well before the Rapa Nui arrived on its shores. This conclusion is supported by geologist such as Robert Shoch, along with numerous other researchers.

Moai facing inland at Ahu Tongariki on Easter Island: Wikipedia

One of the most interesting and mysterious features on Easter Island is the megalithic wall known as Ahu Vinapu, which was built from enormous stone slabs that were laid with great skill. These megalithic blocks were placed so precisely that not even a piece of paper can fit between the stones. The construction techniques used in this wall is unique to the island but is nearly identical to many other megalithic sites found in South America, such as Machu Picchu and Cusco. Not only that, but the Moai statues of Easter Island are also strikingly similar to the Ponce monolith found in Tiwanaku, Bolivia - providing evidence they were all connected in deep antiquity. Could the same influences that gave rise to these giant Moai statues and megalithic walls of Easter Island be connected to not only South America, but also Indonesia and Turkey? Let's go deeper.

Sulawesi, Indonesia

Located in the remote countryside of Indonesia, the Bada Valley of Central Sulawesi contains some of the most enigmatic and peculiar monolithic structures in the world. Discovered in 1908, over 400 granite megaliths are estimated to be scattered throughout the region - yet no official tally for them exists, as no comprehensive archaeological study has ever been done. How old these monoliths are and who the original builders were still remains a mystery. Even experts like Iksam Kailey - the Curator of the Province Museum in Sulawesi, admits that he has no idea when these megaliths were built or what civilizations created them.

Two Dutch ladies standing by a statue in Bada Valley in the 1930s. Wikipedia

In the local Badaic and Indonesian languages, these monoliths are called 'watu arca' which means "stone statues". When inquiring with the indigenous Bugis and Makassarese people of Sulawesi, they state that they have no knowledge of who built these megaliths, only that they have - in their words, "always been there". There are several beliefs held by the indigenous groups of the island regarding the megalithic statues, with some stating that they were created for ancestral worship, or that they may even have supernatural powers - connecting back to ancient gods from long ago.

Out of the more than 400 megaliths in the Bada Valley, around 30 of them depict human-like forms, with the rest being a mixture of mysterious giant bowl-like objects and other strange shapes. The curious thing about the megaliths is that they aren't carved out of any stone found in the area, and likely came from the rugged mountains located several miles away. However, that's just a theory, as no one has ever been able to even find the quarry from which they were created from. Sadly, because there is little protection or record keeping of this site, reports from a census done in 2005 found that at least 60 of these megaliths have been stolen - likely sold on the black market to private collectors.

The most well-known and photographed megalith in the Bada Valley is known as Watu Palindo or simply Palindo, which translates to mean 'the wise man' or 'entertainer' depending on the translation used. According to some local legends, the statue was placed specifically to face the ancient palace of the king, in order to "entertain" him, hence the name. However, its real purpose remains somewhat unknown.

At 15 feet tall, Watu Palindo is the largest megalith in the Bada Valley. Carved out of a single block, it weighs more than 20 tons and depicts a humanoid-like figure that closely resembles both the Moai statues of Easter Island and Ponce monolith of Tiwanaku, Bolivia. The location where this stone was quarried is unknown, as the geology doesn't match anything found in the valley. Sticking out of the ground at an extreme angle, it appears that the megalith was nearly knocked over from an extreme event in the past. In fact, most of the 400 megaliths found throughout the Bada Valley are either knocked over, partially buried, or severely damaged, which provides evidence that they may have been impacted by a massive torrent of water - likely during the Younger Dryas period.

Along with the megalith known as Watu Palinda, there are hundreds of others scattered throughout the Bada Valley. The second largest is known as Maturu, which means "the sleeping statue". At over 11 feet tall, the megalith was found lying on its back, showing that it likely had succumbed to the same event that impacted Watu Palindo - long before it was re-discovered. Some of these megaliths - such as the Baula statue, were found barely sticking above the ground, submerged in flooded rice fields, while others lay half buried in river beds at the edge of the jungle, indicative of how ancient they are and the events they endured.

Besides the mysteries that remain regarding the purpose and creation of the watu statues, there are other structures that are equally as puzzling. Strewn throughout the region, giant bowl-like megaliths known as Kalambas - accompanied by large lids, add another layer to this enigmatic culture. With some weighing over a ton and created with high precision, the Kalambas of the Bada Valley leave many archeologists and researchers scratching their heads with what their purpose could have been. One of the most compelling theories states that they were used as large fermentation containers during important ritualistic ceremonies, centered around the megalithic watu's. This could explain why they were found in such close proximity to one another. Truthfully though, the actual purpose is still unknown.

While many of the megaliths of the Bada Valley resemble humanoids, there are others that seem to depict beings that are not of this world. One has to wonder if the ancient culture that created these statues were depicting the influences of extraterrestrial beings from the stars that gave rise to their civilization in deep antiquity. The evidence to support that theory comes from the numerous similarities we find with other ancient megaliths from around the world - specifically those from Easter Island, Bolivia, and Turkey, all of which seem to depict a powerful influence that created their culture long ago. Could these beings have been the Anunnaki?

The most significant of these similarities leads us back to where we first started, more than 8,000 miles away from Sulawesi, Indonesia with the giant Moai statues of Easter Island. Not only are the megalithic watu statues of Sulawesi similar in appearance to the Moai, but the depictions and symbols carved into them are nearly identical. The most significant of these connections comes in the form of hands that are shown clasping the lower part of the belly - just above the naval, which wasn't discovered until 1914 when they finally excavated them. However, it wasn't until the early 2000's that this information became known outside of certain archaeological circles, seemingly being concealed because of the implications it had for the true age of when they are created.

These depictions found on both the watu statues of Sulawesi and Moai of Easter Island indicate that both of those cultures revered the importance of fertility. We know these symbols represent fertility because of the presence of the phallus shown in between the clasped hands on the watu statues of Sulawesi. The phallus is considered the most important fertility symbol by ancient cultures around the world.

The mystery surrounding the similarities shared between Sulawesi, Indonesia and Easter Island only deepens when one considers the connections that also exist in Tiwanaku, Bolivia with a ten-foot-tall statue known as the Ponce monolith. Not only does it display a similar type of headdress/hat like the statues found on Easter Island and Sulawesi, but the depictions of its hands are also extremely similar. This cannot be simply a coincidence and shows that all of these cultures likely had the same influences thousands of years ago.

Along with the similarities that exist with the statues from Easter Island, Tiwanaku, and Sulawesi, there are other locations around the world that also share the same symbols depicted on those megaliths. Located thousands of miles away in the Anatolia region of Turkey, the ancient celestial temple complex of Gobekli Tepe contains several stone pillars that display the same type of hand depictions as both Easter Island and Sulawesi. Not only that, but seven miles to the southwest of Gobekli Tepe - near the city of Urfa, a mysterious 6-foot-tall stone statue discovered in 1993 known as the "Urfa man" also shows the same depictions.

What makes the Urfa man statue so unique and important are the similarities seen on the lower part of the body with the clasped hands around the phallus. This is nearly identical to the fertility symbols found on the watu statues of Sulawesi and very similar to the Moai of Easter Island, which clearly shows that they were once all connected to the influences of the ancient sages and mystics that came from the civilizations of Lemuria/Mu, and Atlantis.

Conclusion

The similarities and shared characteristics found on the watu statues of Sulawesi, the Moai of Easter Island, Ponce monolith of Tiwanaku, or pillars and statues from Turkey are impossible to ignore. When combined with sunken ruins around the world - such as off Cuba, Greece, Egypt, or India, as well as mathematically precise and highly sophisticated pyramids, megalithic ruins, and temples located on the 30th parallel, a story begins to emerge. This story forms the basis for nearly every legend and sacred text throughout history, that speaks of ancient celestial gods, the rise and fall of grand civilizations, and devastating catastrophes that occur on the Earth every 13,000 years. This cycle led to the collective amnesia of our past that we share today - where over time, society became convinced that the stories of these advanced civilizations and powerful gods were merely myths, causing their legacy to become nearly lost to history, sinking beneath the depths of our own ignorance and conditioning. Will we survive the next cycle of catastrophes on the planet to achieve what no other civilization has before us – learning the truth of who we are and our history? Only time will tell...

Chapter 5 – Unveiling the Matrix of Reality

By Billy Carson

As the chapter begins, we set the scene by emphasizing the enigmatic allure of the ancient world. Humanity's journey through time is marked by a series of forgotten epochs, each holding its own mysteries and wisdom. This chapter proposes a bold hypothesis: that in the annals of our ancient past lies a forgotten key, a key that could unlock the matrix of reality. This matrix, a conceptual framework encompassing the fundamental truths of our existence, remains shrouded in mystery, much like the ancient civilizations that once flourished on Earth. The quest to understand this past is not just a historical endeavor, but rather a venture into the very depths of reality itself, seeking answers to questions that have perplexed humanity since time immemorial.

We then delve into the rich tapestry of ancient civilizations, exploring how their understanding of the world might offer clues to this hidden matrix. From the philosophical musings of Ancient Greece to the cosmic insights of Mayan astronomers, each culture offered a unique perspective on the nature of reality. These ancient societies were not just primitive predecessors of our modern age but were repositories of profound knowledge and understanding, some of which are only now being rediscovered and appreciated. Their monumental structures, intricate art, and enduring literature suggest a deep connection with aspects of reality that modern science is only beginning to grasp.

The narrative shifts to explore the concept of the matrix of reality. This matrix is not a physical structure but an abstract, multidimensional framework that underpins all existence. It's a fusion of the physical and metaphysical, where matter, energy, consciousness, and the laws of nature coalesce. With their holistic view of the universe, the ancients might have had insights into this matrix that modern civilization, with its fragmented approach to knowledge, overlooked. By studying ancient philosophies, sacred geometries, and esoteric teachings, we can piece together a more comprehensive understanding of the universe, an understanding that transcends the limitations of our current scientific paradigms.

The chapter concludes by emphasizing the significance of this exploration for the future of humanity. Understanding the matrix of reality as perceived by our ancestors could fundamentally alter our perception of existence, leading to advancements in technology, philosophy, and spirituality. By reexamining and integrating the wisdom of the past, we might unveil a more profound truth about our universe, a truth that could propel humanity toward a new era of enlightenment and discovery, where the mysteries of existence are not only pondered but also understood.

In the King James Version (KJV) of the Bible, the term "matrix" is used in its archaic sense to mean "womb," particularly in the context of laws pertaining to the firstborn, as seen in books like Exodus. This straightforward, literal interpretation contrasts sharply with the richly layered, metaphysical implications of the term as popularized by the "Matrix" movie series. In the films, the Matrix represents a simulated reality, a complex, artificial world designed to mask an underlying truth. This cinematic portrayal echoes deeper philosophical and spiritual themes, resonating with the idea of a reality beyond our immediate perception. While the biblical use of "matrix" is grounded in the physical aspect of birth and life, the movie catapults the term into existential questioning and the search for fundamental truth, bridging ancient text and contemporary thought in a unique juxtaposition of meanings and interpretations.

"Matrix" in the Bible

Exo 13:12
Tools

> *That thou shalt set apart unto the LORD all that openeth the matrix, and every firstling that cometh of a beast which thou hast; the males shall be the LORD'S.*

KJV
Verse Concepts
Exo 13:15
Tools

And it came to pass, when Pharaoh would hardly let us go, that the LORD slew all the firstborn in the land of Egypt, both the firstborn of man, and the firstborn of beast: therefore I sacrifice to the LORD all that openeth the matrix, being males; but all the firstborn of my children I redeem.

KJV
Verse Concepts
Exo 34:19
Tools

All that openeth the matrix is mine; and every firstling among thy cattle, whether ox or sheep, that is male.

KJV
Verse Concepts
Num 3:12
Tools

And I, behold, I have taken the Levites from among the children of Israel instead of all the firstborn that openeth the matrix among the children of Israel: therefore the Levites shall be mine;

KJV
Verse Concepts
Num 18:15
Tools

Every thing that openeth the matrix in all flesh, which they bring unto the LORD, whether it be of men or beasts, shall be thine:

> *nevertheless the firstborn of man shalt thou surely redeem, and the firstling of unclean beasts shalt thou redeem.*

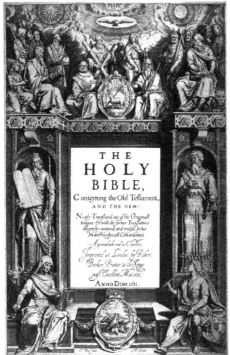

King James Version Of The Bible: Wikipedia

The passage referred to here comes from the Bible, specifically Exodus 13:12. In this verse, the Lord instructs the Israelites to set apart for Him every firstborn that opens the womb, both from their livestock and other animals. The firstborn males were to be dedicated to the Lord.

This commandment was part of the larger context of the Israelites' exodus from Egypt. The Lord had just delivered them from slavery and performed various miracles, including the final plague of the death of the firstborn in Egypt. As a commemoration of their deliverance and a recognition of the

Lord's ownership and authority over all things, the firstborn males were to be consecrated to Him.

It is worth noting that the Hebrew word for "matrix" in this context refers to the womb or the opening of the womb. So, any firstborn male that came from the womb of an animal was to be set apart for the Lord.

This commandment played a significant role in the religious practices of ancient Israel and was later expanded upon in the laws and rituals of the Mosaic covenant.

In the movie "The Matrix," the character Neo, played by Keanu Reeves, exits the Matrix through a process called "jacking out" or "being unplugged." The Matrix is depicted as a simulated reality created by artificial intelligence to control and manipulate human beings while their physical bodies are kept in a state of unconsciousness to act as batteries to power the machines.

Neo, initially unaware of the true nature of reality, is contacted by a group of rebels led by Morpheus. They believe that Neo is "The One," a prophesied figure who has the potential to free humanity from the Matrix. They teach him about the true nature of the world and its simulated reality.

To exit the Matrix, Neo is connected to a special device called a "jack" or "port," which allows him to establish a neural connection with the Matrix. This connection enables him to perceive and interact with the virtual environment. The rebels then use another device to physically disconnect him from the Matrix while his consciousness remains intact.

During his first "jacking out" experience, Neo is taken to a designated location within the Matrix called a "construct," where he meets Morpheus and his crew in their real-world form. From there, he is physically extracted from the pod in which his physical body was kept captive, and he wakes up in the real world.

Throughout the movie, Neo learns to manipulate the Matrix, gaining superhuman abilities within the simulated reality. This allows him to bend the rules of the Matrix, ultimately leading to his ability to enter and exit the Matrix at will, empowering him to confront the agents and challenge the system.

The term "neocortex" refers to a part of the brain. The neocortex is the outermost layer of the cerebral cortex and is responsible for higher cognitive functions, including sensory perception, motor commands, spatial reasoning, conscious thought, and language processing.

The neocortex is found in mammals and is particularly well-developed in humans compared to other species. It is divided into different regions, each associated with specific functions. These regions include the frontal lobe, parietal lobe, temporal lobe, and occipital lobe.

The neocortex is highly interconnected with other parts of the brain, such as the limbic system, which is involved in emotions and memory, and the basal ganglia, which plays a role in movement control and habit formation. Its intricate structure and extensive neural connections enable complex information processing, learning, and the ability to adapt to new situations.

Overall, the neocortex is a crucial component of the human brain, contributing to our advanced cognitive abilities and playing a fundamental role in various aspects of human experience and behavior.

Unveiling the Matrix of Reality

As we delve deeper into the intricacies of our world, it becomes increasingly evident that parallels can be drawn between our reality and the captivating world portrayed in "The Matrix" film series. While we may not be physically trapped in a simulated construct controlled by machines, there are thought-provoking similarities that warrant exploration. In this chapter, we will embark on a journey to unravel the striking resemblances between our real world and the Matrix.

Perceived Reality vs. Actual Reality:

In "The Matrix," humans exist in a simulated reality, oblivious to the true state of the world. Similarly, in our own lives, we often perceive reality through various filters such as societal norms, cultural beliefs, and personal biases. The information we receive shapes our experiences and perceptions, creating a subjective understanding of the world. Just as the Matrix fabricates a convincing illusion, our own reality can be distorted by misinformation, manipulation, and limited perspectives.

Illusion of Control:

In the Matrix, the machines exert total control over the simulated world, dictating the lives and actions of its inhabitants. In our reality, external influences such as governments, corporations, and social structures can exert significant control over our lives. We are constantly bombarded with subtle influences, propaganda, and societal expectations that shape our behavior and choices, often without us being fully aware of them. This illusory sense of control masks the underlying mechanisms at play.

Information Manipulation:

One of the central themes in the Matrix series is the manipulation of information. Similarly, information manipulation has become a prevalent concern in our interconnected digital age. News media, social media algorithms, and online platforms can filter, distort, and control the information we receive, shaping our perceptions of events and individuals. This selective presentation of reality can lead to a distorted worldview, just as the Matrix architects manipulate the perceptions of its simulated inhabitants.

Questioning Reality:

The protagonist, Neo, begins to question the nature of reality and seeks answers beyond the confines of the Matrix. Similarly, in our world, an increasing number of individuals are questioning the underlying fabric of our reality. Philosophical inquiries, scientific discoveries, and spiritual exploration all contribute to a deeper understanding of our existence. The search for truth and a desire to break free from societal constraints echo Neo's journey of self-discovery and liberation.

Awakening and Transformation:

In "The Matrix," Neo undergoes a transformative journey from a regular individual to a powerful liberator. Likewise, in our lives, moments of awakening can occur when we question our reality and challenge conventional wisdom. These awakenings may lead to personal growth, expanded consciousness, and a realization of our true potential. Just as Neo develops extraordinary abilities within the Matrix, we, too, can tap into hidden capacities and break free from self-imposed limitations.

While we may not be living in a literal Matrix, the film series serves as a metaphor for the deeper truths and hidden dynamics that shape our world. By recognizing the parallels between our reality and the Matrix, we are encouraged to question, explore, and strive for a more authentic understanding of our existence. The journey toward liberation, self-discovery, and the pursuit of truth becomes a shared experience that transcends the boundaries of fiction, echoing the eternal quest for meaning and freedom in our own lives.

Becoming conscious and aware of who you truly are bears a striking resemblance to Neo's journey of escaping the Matrix in several profound ways. Just as Neo discovers the illusionary nature of his reality and seeks liberation, the process of self-discovery and self-awareness can lead to a transformative experience in our own lives.

Breaking Free from Illusions:

Neo's initial realization that the world he thought was real is, in fact, a simulated construct parallels the moment of awakening in our own lives. Similarly, as we embark on a journey of self-discovery, we start to question the beliefs, assumptions, and societal norms that have shaped our identity. We recognize the illusions that have governed our thinking and open ourselves to the possibility of a greater truth beyond the surface level.

Challenging Limiting Beliefs:

Both Neo and individuals on a path of self-awareness encounter limiting beliefs that hold them back. Neo is initially skeptical of his potential as "The One" and struggles to fully embrace his true nature. Similarly, we often carry deep-rooted beliefs about ourselves that restrict our growth and potential. Through self-reflection and exploration, we challenge these self-imposed limitations and begin to recognize our inherent power and possibilities.

Embracing Authenticity:

Neo's journey involves shedding the false persona imposed by the Matrix and embracing his authentic self. In parallel, our own path of self-awareness encourages us to peel away the layers of social conditioning and external expectations. As we gain deeper insights into our true essence, we become more comfortable embracing our authentic selves, free from the need for external validation or conformity. It is a journey of accepting and celebrating our unique qualities, talents, and passions.

Expanding Consciousness:

Neo's growth within the Matrix allows him to transcend the limitations of the simulated world and access heightened levels of consciousness. Similarly, as we become more self-aware, our consciousness expands beyond the confines of our conditioned thinking. We develop a deeper understanding of our thoughts, emotions, and patterns of behavior. This expanded consciousness enables us to make conscious choices, respond to challenges with greater clarity, and connect with a broader sense of purpose and interconnectedness.

Liberating Self and Others:

Neo's ultimate goal is not only to liberate himself but also to free others from the control of the Matrix. Similarly, as we deepen our self-awareness, we cultivate compassion, empathy, and a desire to contribute to the well-being of others. We recognize that our journey of self-discovery is intertwined with the collective journey of humanity. By sharing our insights, inspiring others, and promoting positive change, we actively participate in the liberation of not only ourselves but also those around us.

The Awakening of Higher Consciousness:

In the vast expanse of human existence, there are moments when ordinary life transcends into something extraordinary—a state of being that defies conventional understanding and brings us closer to the profound essence of existence. This is the realm of higher consciousness, a plane where the boundaries of the self dissolve, and we glimpse the interconnectedness of all things.

The awakening of higher consciousness marks the commencement of a remarkable journey—a transformative pilgrimage into the very core of our being. It begins with a subtle whisper, a call from the depths of our soul, beckoning us to explore the mysteries of life beyond the surface. This spiritual yearning awakens a thirst for knowledge, truth, and self-discovery, propelling us on a quest to uncover the profound secrets that lie within.

Across the span of history, spiritual traditions and philosophical teachings have alluded to this state of awakened awareness. From the ancient wisdom of Eastern philosophies like Buddhism and Hinduism to the mystical traditions of Sufism and Kabbalah, the concept of higher consciousness has found expression in various forms across cultures and epochs. It is the common thread that weaves through the tapestry of human spiritual evolution.

In the pursuit of higher consciousness, seekers often embark on a path of self-exploration, diving deep into their own psyche and peeling back the layers of conditioned beliefs and societal expectations. This process of introspection is not for the faint of heart, for it demands the courage to confront our deepest fears, insecurities, and unresolved emotions—the shadows that lurk in the recesses of our subconscious.

As the seeker perseveres through the dark night of the soul, a transformative metamorphosis occurs. The once-limited perception of reality expands, and the veils of ignorance begin to lift. We develop a profound sense of empathy and compassion for all living beings, recognizing that we are interconnected and interdependent in this cosmic dance of existence.

In the realm of higher consciousness, the ego, that ever-present voice of self-centered desires and attachments, takes a back seat. It no longer governs our thoughts, emotions, and actions. Instead, a new sense of self-awareness arises—a witness consciousness that observes the play of life without entanglement. We become co-creators with the universe, aligning our intentions with the greater good and surrendering to the flow of life.

The process of awakening is not a linear path but rather an ever-unfolding spiral of growth and expansion. It requires humility, as the more we learn, the more we realize how much we don't know. It is a dance between seeking knowledge and surrendering to the inherent wisdom that resides within each of us.

Through the practice of meditation, mindfulness, and self-reflection, we cultivate a profound connection to our true essence—the eternal consciousness that transcends the transient fluctuations of thoughts and emotions. In moments of stillness, we touch the vastness of our being, recognizing that we are not separate entities but rather manifestations of the same divine essence that permeates the entire universe.

As the awakening deepens, the old self begins to dissolve, making way for the birth of a new and authentic self. This rebirth is not a one-time event but an ongoing process of growth and refinement. It is the integration of higher consciousness into our daily lives—a harmonious blending of the spiritual and the material, the sacred and the mundane.

With the rebirth of higher consciousness, our relationships, work, and daily interactions undergo a profound transformation. We approach life with a sense of wonder and gratitude, recognizing each moment as a precious gift to be savored. Our actions become guided by compassion and love as we strive to contribute positively to the well-being of others and the world at large.

In conclusion, the philosophy of being born again from a state of higher consciousness is an extraordinary journey of self-discovery and spiritual awakening. It is a call to transcend the limitations of our conditioned minds and embrace the vastness of our true essence. Through the practice of mindfulness, self-reflection, and surrender, we embark on a transformative pilgrimage that leads us to a profound rebirth—a rebirth into the boundless realms of awakened awareness.

In essence, the process of becoming conscious and aware of who we truly are mirrors Neo's escape from the Matrix. It involves breaking free from illusions, challenging limiting beliefs, embracing authenticity, expanding consciousness, and actively participating in the liberation of ourselves and others. Both journeys are transformative, empowering, and offer the potential for a profound shift in how we experience and engage with the world.

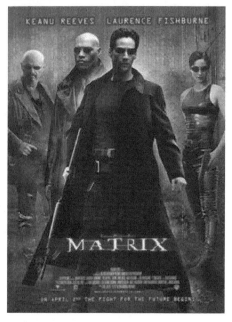

Theatrical release poster "The Matrix" Wikipedia

Understanding the matrix of reality as perceived by our ancestors is not merely an academic pursuit. It's a journey that could fundamentally alter our perception of existence, leading to advancements in technology, philosophy, and spirituality. By reexamining and integrating the wisdom of the past, we might unveil a more profound truth about our universe, a truth that could propel humanity toward a new era of enlightenment and discovery, where the mysteries of existence are not only contemplated but also understood.

The Authors

Matthew LaCroix (Best Selling Author)

Matthew LaCroix is a passionate writer and researcher who grew up exploring the outdoors of northern New England. After college, he began studying ancient civilizations, philosophy, quantum mechanics, and history. His focus became uncovering and connecting the esoteric teachings from secret societies and ancient cultures that disappeared long ago. At 32 he published his first major book: The Illusion of Us, which combined years of research to discover the truth about the past, human origins, the gods of antiquity, as well as the fundamentals of consciousness.

In 2019 he released his second book entitled: The Stage of Time, which represents a compilation of studying ancient texts, evidence for lost civilizations, spiritual wisdom, and theoretical physics, combined together to find answers to some of our most difficult questions.

Matthew was as a writer and researcher at Gaia and has appeared on shows such as Ancient Civilizations on Gaia, The UnXplained on the History Channel, and Mystery School of Truth on 4Biddenknowledge TV. He is also a frequent guest on numerous podcasts and radio shows. In 2022 he released his third major book written with Billy Carson entitled: The Epic of Humanity, which focuses on uncovering the mysteries of the human story, the timeline of lost civilizations, and ancient catastrophes.

Billy Carson (Best Selling Author)

Billy Carson is the founder and CEO of 4BiddenKnowledge Inc, and the Best Selling Author of The Compendium Of The Emerald Tablets and Woke Doesn't Mean Broke.

Mr. Carson is also the founder and CEO of 4BiddenKnowledge TV, a new conscious streaming TV network on Apple TV, Roku, Amazon Fire TV, iOS, GooglePlay and the web, the Co-Host of Bio-Hack Your Best Life, and is an expert host on 'Anunnaki Ancient Secrets Revealed' an exclusive 4biddenknowledge TV series. Mr. Carson has also appeared on Deep Space, an original streaming series by Gaia. This series explores the Secret Space Program, revealing extraordinary technologies and their potential origins. Mr. Carson also serves as an expert host on Gaia's original series, Ancient Civilizations, in which a team of renowned scholars deciphers the riddles of our origins and pieces together our forgotten history documented in monuments and texts around the world.

Mr. Carson appreciates the dedication and hard work it takes to accomplish great things. Recently, Mr. Carson earned the Certificate of Science (with an emphasis on Neuroscience) at M.I.T. and has a certificate in Ancient Civilization from Harvard University. Among his most notable achievements, Billy is the CEO of First Class Space Agency based in Fort Lauderdale, FL. Specifically, his space agency is involved in research and development of alternative propulsion systems, zero-point energy devices and other technologies that can change the world.

Made in United States
Orlando, FL
30 December 2023